To: Kevin Ashl... *[barcode: W9-DDY-871]*

University of Georgia

1993

From: Trinity United Methodist Women
Jenny Springer, Pres.

E. Herbert Franklin, Minister.

Can You Remember to Forget?

Can You Remember to Forget?

And 3² Other Questions for Tomorrow's Leaders

James W. Moore

ABINGDON PRESS
Nashville

CAN YOU REMEMBER TO FORGET?
AND 32 OTHER QUESTIONS FOR TOMORROW'S LEADERS

Copyright © 1991 by Abingdon Press
Second Printing 1993
All rights reserved.

This book is printed on recycled acid-free paper.

Library of Congress Cataloging-in-Publication Data

Moore, James W. 1938–
    Can you remember to forget? : and 32 other questions for tomorrow's leaders / James W. Moore.
        p.   cm.
    ISBN 0-687-04628-9 (alk. paper)
    1. Young adults—Religious life. 2. Leadership—Religious aspects—Christianity. 3. College graduates—Religious life. 4. High school graduates—Religious life. I. Title.
BV4529.2.M66   1991
248.8'3—dc20   91-24376

"Pronouns" from *Burning Bush* by Karle Wilson Baker (p. 62-63), copyright 1922 by Yale University Press, is used by permission of the copyright holder.

"Outwitted" by Edwin Markham (p. 44), copyright renewal 1930 by the author, is used by permission of the Markham Archives, Wagner College, Staten Island, N.Y.

Scripture quotations noted NEB are from The New English Bible © The Delegates of the Oxford University Press and The Syndics of the Cambridge University Press 1961, 1970. Reprinted by permission.

Those noted Phillips are from The New Testament in Modern English, Rev. Ed., by J. B. Phillips. Copyright © J. B. Phillips, 1958, 1959, 1960, 1972. Reprinted by permission of The Macmillan Co.

Those noted RSV are from the Revised Standard Version of the Bible, copyright 1946, 1952, 1971 by the Division of Christian Education of the national Council of Churches of Christ in the U.S.A. Used by permissions.

Those note KJV are from the King James Version of the Bible.

Many Scripture quotations are the author's own version.

For my family at home,
for my family at church,
for my special friends,
and especially for the thoughtful young people
who have walked into my life and helped me
with some of life's poignant questions

Contents

Introduction

Faith Is the Answer, But What Are the Questions?

Recently I ran across a fascinating list of unusual answers given by children on some school tests.

- In answer to the question, "When was our nation founded?" one little boy wrote, "I didn't even know it was losted!"

- Another said that Socrates died from an overdose of "wedlock"!

- Asked to describe the famous painting of Whistler's mother, one student explained: "It shows a nice little lady sitting in a chair, waiting for the repairman to bring back her TV set!"

- And then, how about these interesting answers:

  "A horse divided against itself can't stand"!

  "The death of Thomas Jefferson was a big turning point in his life"!

  "Zanzibar is noted for its monkeys; the British governor lives there"!

- Here is my favorite: A little girl was asked to define the word *people,* and this is what she wrote: "People are composed of girls and boys and men and women. Girls are nice. Boys are no good until they are grown up and married. My mother is a woman, which is a grown-up girl with children. My father is so nice that I think he must have been a girl when he was a boy"!

We can tell from these amusing classroom responses that right answers are important. But have you thought about this: The right *questions* are important, too! How essential it is to match the right answers with the right questions! And nowhere is this more important than in the realm of religion. It is common these days to see bumper stickers, posters, lapel buttons, and highway signs that display the words Faith Is the Answer.

Of course, as Christians, we believe this to be true. We believe that faith indeed is the answer, but these words must be more than a religious cliché or a pious platitude. The serious thinker won't let us get away with snappy slogans. The serious thinker comes back and asks: "What are the questions?"

"If faith is the answer, what are the questions?" We do need to consider this, because the only way we can make our answer relevant and meaningful is to relate that answer to the proper questions.

Math books sometimes have the answers printed in the back of the book. You can always get the right answer, but the answers by themselves mean nothing. They become significant and meaningful only when they are related to the specific problems in the textbook. Only then does learning and growth take place. It isn't enough to know the answers. You also need to know the question.

And that's what this book is about—"life" answers related to "life" questions:

- What does it really mean to be a Christian?
- Can you remember to forget?
- What does it mean to be good?

10

- Can your conscience be your guide?
- How does faith mend a broken heart?
- What is the one thing that is always right?

These questions and many more are examined here. This is the way we grow and mature—by raising questions and struggling with them.

Psychologists tell us that as long as we live, we will have two conflicting desires working within us and grappling for our allegiance. One desire is the temptation to quit on life, to throw in the towel and give in to boredom and closedmindedness. The other desire is the determination to move forward, to struggle, to discover, with open minds, more and more of God's truth.

Of course, the Christian faith calls us to move forward, to join the struggle, to raise the questions and face them head-on. Good questions are not stumbling blocks; they are stepping-stones to God's truth.

Should You Raise Questions About Faith?

Is it wrong to wonder? Is it sinful to doubt? Is it bad to raise questions about our faith?

In *Spiritual Autobiography,* Dr. William Barclay says that some people are what you might call "natural believers"—that belief is easier for some people than it is for others. On the other hand, some people find it extremely hard to believe, and I guess all of us have moments when we want to cry out, with the man in the Gospels, "Lord, I believe; help thou my unbelief!"

What about you? Is it easy or hard for you to believe? Do you ever feel that your faith is not as strong as you would like it to be? There is a story in Mark 9 about a father who is worried sick because for several years his son has been having terrible seizures which render him speechless—awful convulsions which knock him to the ground and cause him to foam at the mouth, grind his teeth, go rigid all over. Imagine the concern of this father. He has tried everything. He wants so much for his son to be made well.

He brings him to Jesus and says, "Please help us, if you can."

Jesus answers, "If you can! All things are possible for him who believes!"

Note the desperation of that father as he cries out, "I believe; help thou my unbelief!" In other words, "I'm believing as much as I can—please make up for my inadequate faith." Then Mark tells us that Jesus heals the boy.

My heart goes out to that father and to people like him who want so much to believe but find it difficult to do so. What can we say to these people? What do *we* do when we come to a place in life where it is hard to believe? Let me suggest a few things to remember.

First, remember that our beliefs may be challenged.

We can't permit ourselves to be so insecure that we are shaken by every ripple or confusion or question. The truth is that sometimes these challenges are stepping-stones to growth. They force us to think through our beliefs more seriously.

Sometimes challenges to our beliefs are painful, but "growing pains" seem to be an inevitable part of maturing. *God gave us minds, and surely God meant for us to use them.* I have never known mature Christians who, at some point, did not raise questions about their faith and then set out to find the answers.

I have a minister friend who purposefully listens to a radio preacher with whom he disagrees. They are poles apart theologically. Their approaches to faith are completely different. My friend listens to that preacher as a discipline in thinking, asking himself, "Why do I see that differently? What do I really believe about this? Why is my approach different?" He says this exercise has helped him reach fresh new insights in the Christian faith.

The point is clear: Our faith should not stifle our questions, and our questions should not stifle our faith. Rather, questions may be the means by which our faith grows and deepens.

Second, when it's hard to believe,
remember the people who believe.

Remember the great cloud of witnesses, the company of the committed. The most fulfilled, productive, creative, joyous people I know about have been *believers,* and that is reassuring. Think of Abraham, Moses, David, Jeremiah, Isaiah, Peter, Paul, Luther, Calvin, Wesley, Francis of Assisi, Mother Teresa, Bonhoeffer, Tillich, Von Braun, Livingston, Brooks, Schweitzer, the people in your congregation, and

Jesus of Nazareth. I'd like to take my stand with Jesus and with them.

Third, when it's hard to believe,
remember the church.

Remember what it is, what it represents, what it can be. Would you want to live where there is no church? No! Because at its best, the church represents the best there is in this world. I know the church has its weaknesses, but I also wish I had more than one life to give to the church.

Fourth, when it's hard to believe,
remember that doubts about nonessentials
can blind us to the essentials.

Some people worry about things that don't matter and thereby miss the things that do matter very much. Does it really make any difference what clothes we wear or what type car we drive? We can toy with nonessentials and miss the important things, such as honesty, integrity, truth, faith, hope, love, and kindness.

Fifth, when it's hard to believe, remember
that faith is confirmed by the living of it.

Faith is strengthened by practice. Jesus didn't tell us to memorize the doctrines. He said, "Follow me"!

Do You Have a Bad Case of the Religious Simples?

Some years ago, the late Senator Thomas Hart Benton was asked about the most difficult aspect of being a United States Senator. His answer was interesting. He said that, for him, the hardest thing to deal with was the frustrating fact that his constituents in Missouri had a "bad case of the simples"! That is, they expected him to work instant miracles in Washington. They reduced all complexities to neat little black-and-white simplicities. They didn't seem to realize that the most meaningful and significant accomplishments take time, effort, commitment, sacrifice, discipline, and perseverance.

Senator Benton was on target. The fact is that nothing in this world is simple, if by simple we mean easy to grasp—nothing! A blade of grass is not a simple thing, nor is a teardrop or a snowflake or an atom or an electron or love. As someone once said, "Take three steps into anything, and you are over your head in an ocean of mystery."

I recently read about a man who wanted a revelation from God: "I want a revelation. I want God to speak to me simple and straight."

Finally his pastor said to him, "The next time it rains, go outside, look up into the heavens, and ask God for a revelation."

A few days later, after a good soaking rain, the man came back to his pastor. He was sopping wet.

"I followed your advice," he said. "I stood in the rain for over an hour, looking up into the skies and asking for a revelation from God, but no revelation came. The rain pelted my face, the water ran down my neck, and I felt ignorant and stupid."

The pastor replied, "What greater revelation do you want?"

Most of us don't need to stand in the rain to realize how ignorant we are in this complex universe. Even Thomas Edison, as knowledgeable as he was, said, "We don't know the millionth part of one percent about anything."

So there's no use asking for a simple religion:

> I don't know who first coined the phrase "The Simple Gospel." I hope that God, being slow to anger and plenteous in mercy has forgiven them, but the evil they did lives after them. For hiding under that innocent phrase, "The Simple Gospel," is usually a distorted, deluded message picking out a few factors and leaving out all the rest. (J. Wallace Hamilton, *Where Now Is Thy God?* p. 115)

We must beware of oversimplification. We must beware of the "religious simples." The things that matter most in life do not come quickly, easily, or simply; they take time, effort, sacrifice, and commitment. To be sure, you can get some things immediately by pushing buttons or paying money down or pulling out a plastic card. But the great things, the real values, do not come that way. They have to be grown and cultivated. You can obtain a sports car or a color TV with a quick down payment, but you must wait for, long for, commit to, and slowly but surely grow into, character, morality, values, faith, maturity, and spiritual strength.

For example, it is no simple matter to develop a meaningful prayer life. It doesn't happen overnight. It doesn't appear instantly or magically. It takes a lot of time and a lot of practice. Florence Allshorn said, "There is really only one test of our prayer life. Namely, do we want God? Do we want Him so much that we'll go on and on if it takes five, six, ten years to find Him?" (*The Healing Fountain*, p. 15). If you want to become a doctor, lawyer, minister, teacher, musician or an athlete, it takes effort and determination. It doesn't come easily or simply. Maybe the same is true with prayer. Maybe it just takes a lot of practice.

And it is no simple matter to develop a meaningful understanding of the Scriptures. The truth is that while the Bible is in nearly all our homes, not all of us are at home in the Bible, as Edward Blair points out in *The Bible and You*:

> The person who is looking for a way to master the Bible in three easy lessons will be disappointed . . . In the first place one can never master the Bible; one can only be mastered by it. In the second place, the Bible is so incalculably rich that the human mind cannot possibly embrace it all in a few attempts. . . . Familiarity with the Bible comes only by long exposure to its contents. (p. 52)

So it is no simple matter to be a faithful Christian. It is a growing, developing thing. It is not a single act or event, an experience suddenly over and done with. It is a wonderful thing to become "new born"—but to remain a spiritual baby is tragic. Babies are sweet and adorable, but if they never grow up, we consider that a calamity—and it is. Becoming a faithful Christian is an ongoing process, a pilgrimage, a life commitment. It is not simple or easy. We need to practice, practice, practice!

What Does It Really Mean to Be Christian?

From the story of the rich young ruler in the Gospel of Mark (10:17-22), we can learn, in a back-door kind of way, the key characteristics of Christian discipleship—what it means to be Christian, or Christ-like.

Jesus is on his way to Jerusalem (and the cross), when the rich young ruler runs up and kneels before him. Notice this: He runs up (a sign of enthusiasm); he kneels down (a sign of respect and reverence). So we can assume that this young man is not trying to trap Jesus with loaded questions, but that he is sincere when he asks, "Good teacher, what must I do to inherit eternal life?"

Jesus answers, "You know the commandments: Do not kill; do not commit adultery; do not steal or defraud or bear false witness; honor your father and mother."

The young man responds, "All these I have kept from my youth."

Jesus then looks at him with love and says, "You lack one thing; go, sell what you own, and give the money to the poor, and you will have treasure in heaven; then come, follow me." Upon hearing this, the rich young ruler turns away and leaves sorrowfully, for he is a wealthy man.

In the young man's failure to respond and follow Jesus, we find some basic insights into what it means to be Christian.

First, a Christian is one who sees God through the eyes of Christ.

That's the key thing about Jesus. He shows us what God is like. He gives God a face, and that face is love. A few years ago, I was interviewing John Killinger on a TV talk show, and he put it like this: "Jesus was God's way of getting rid of a bad reputation!" Isn't that a great quote? Jesus came to show us that God is not an angry and hostile deity, not an impersonal cosmic force, but a loving father, a God of love and compassion who cares for all his children. Notice in the Gospels how many times Jesus says, "Fear not!" or "Don't be afraid!" We don't need to be afraid of God, or of life and its

19

problems and challenges, because God is with us to see us through. The rich young ruler didn't understand this. Frightened, he turned away.

Second, a Christian is one who sees value through the eyes of Christ.

In the rich young ruler incident, Christ gives us a new way of looking at things, a new way to measure what is important, a new scale of values. Sometimes we stress the rich young ruler's lack of commitment so much that we miss one of the key insights of this story—namely, Christ's way of measuring what is valuable!

Here is a man who is rich materially. He is young, a success, a ruler, a leader; he has it all—wealth, youth, power. Yet here is the point: Despite all that, there is something missing—a void, an emptiness, a hunger. Jesus sees right to the heart of it: "One thing you lack." Jesus is not denouncing wealth. Rather, he is saying, "Following me is the greatest treasure in the world. It is wealth beyond counting." Jesus is talking not only about the cost of discipleship, but about the *riches* of discipleship. He is saying that discipleship is better than dollars. It's the top priority, the most important and the most valuable thing in the world!

Third, a Christian is one who sees other people through the eyes of Christ.

The keynote of Christ's life and ministry was his concern for others, his love for other people. Notice how this love for others is underscored in the rich young ruler story. Not only does Christ tell the young man to care for the poor and needy, but when he talks about the Commandments, he mentions only those that concern our relationships with other people. What do you make of that? There is no mention of love for

God. Why? Well, simply because this is the way we express our love for God best—by loving other people! As a friend once put it: "When I first became a Christian, I was so excited, I wanted to hug God. Over the years, I have learned that the way you hug God is to hug his people!"

Fourth, a Christian is one who sees life through the eyes of Christ.

When we look at life through the eyes of Christ, two things stand out—urgency and self-giving. The rich young ruler missed that. Yet this is what Jesus had in mind when he said, "The Kingdom is at hand"—that is, "Now is the time to serve the King of Kings!" In fact, we could well describe Christ's life as "urgent self-giving." He saw every moment, every experience, every encounter, every interruption as a unique and urgent opportunity to give himself for others.

That's what it means to be a Christian—to serve God and give ourselves for the cause of Christ in every moment; to see every day and every occasion as a special and urgent opportunity to be like Christ, to continue his message, his work, his love. Or as my friend Don Webb puts it, "to have Christed-eyes"!

How Did Jesus Picture God?

Tony Orlando's recording of the song "Tie a Yellow Ribbon 'Round the Old Oak Tree" was a big hit in the 1970s. And the song lives on, as evidenced by the nationwide display of yellow ribbons during the 1990s crisis in the Persian Gulf.

As you listen to the words of the song, you can picture a young man who has been away from his wife or girlfriend for three long years. Now he is coming home, but he doesn't know what kind of reception awaits him. After the hurt and heartache he has caused, he doesn't know how welcome he will be, so he has sent a message ahead: "If you still love me, if you forgive me, tie a yellow ribbon around the oak tree. If I see the ribbon, I'll get off the bus; if not, I'll stay on the bus and be out of your life." But when he arrives, he sees a hundred yellow ribbons 'round the old oak tree!

Now I have a strong suspicion that this song was inspired by an old story that preachers have loved to tell for many generations. Such obvious similarities just couldn't be a coincidence. See what you think.

The old story takes place on a train (rather than a bus). The young man has been away from his family (rather than a girlfriend). The tree is a crabapple tree (rather than an old oak tree). The signal is a white rag, rather than a yellow ribbon. Except for those minor differences, the homiletical story is almost identical to the popular song. It goes like this.

A young man was on a train. He seemed deeply troubled, nervous, anxious, afraid. He was fighting back the tears. An older man seated beside him sensed that something was wrong and asked the younger man if he was all right. The young man, needing to talk, blurted out his story: Three years before, after an argument with his father, the young man had run away from home. He had chased back and forth across the country, looking for freedom and happiness, and with every passing day, had become more miserable. Finally it dawned on him that, more than anything, home was where he wanted to be. But he didn't know how his parents felt about him now. After all, he had hurt them deeply. He had said some cruel, callous things to his father. He had left an arrogant note on his pillow. He wouldn't blame them if they never wanted to see him again. He had written ahead that he would be passing by the backyard on the afternoon train on this day. If they forgave him, if they wanted to see him, if they wanted him to come home, they were to tie a white rag on the crabapple tree in the backyard. If he saw the white rag, he would get off the train and come home; if not, he would stay on the train.

Just as the young man finished his story, the train began to slow down as it pulled into the town where his family lived. Tension was so heavy, the young man couldn't bear to look.

The older man said, "I'll watch for you. Put your head down and relax. Close your eyes. I'll watch for you!"

As they came to the old home place, the older man looked, and then excitedly touched the young man on the shoulder.

"Look, son, look! You can go home! You can go home! There's a white rag on every limb!"

Isn't that a great story? The truth is that this powerful story is simply a modern retelling of the greatest short story in history—Jesus' parable of the prodigal son! That parable is not well-named because it actually is about a father and two sons. Besides, the real hero is the father, not the prodigal. In the father, we see the central truth that Jesus wanted to communicate through the story. It probably should be called the parable of the loving father.

Justifiably, this parable has been called the greatest short story in the world because it is packed with the stuff of life. It has everything:

- *Powerful Symbols:* the robe, the ring, the shoes, the inheritance, the feast, the pigs, the far country.
- *Provocative Drama:* a fascinating interplay of emotions: love and jealousy, tenderness and rebellion, acceptance and rejection, compassion and envy, humility and arrogance.
- *Deep Theological Understanding:* sin, repentance, grace, forgiveness.

All of that is there, and more. Most important, though, there we have the picture of how Jesus saw God and how Jesus understood God to be. If Jesus had been a painter, and if he had painted a picture of God, he would have painted him boldly and tenderly as a *loving father!*

What is the point of the parable? The theme of this parable is not the revelry of the prodigal, nor is it the bitterness of the elder brother. The theme is the goodness of the father, the faithfulness of the father; the grace of God. The message here is "good news"—that God cares about all his sons. The father wants both sons to come to the feast. The father wants both sons to join the party. The father wants both sons to be a part of the merry-making. The father wants both sons to eat at his table. The father wants all his children to come, hand-in-hand, to his celebration!

What Does It Mean to Be Good?

What does it mean to be good? Over the years, this important question has been answered by a variety of people in a variety of ways. Broadly speaking, the answers may be summed up in four categories or responses.

First, there are the excuse-makers.

In answer to the question, "What does it mean to be good?" some make excuses; they try to rationalize the problem away. The problem of immorality, private and public, has always been with us, but today it is different. No longer do we try to hide our sins. Now we giggle about them, rationalize them, excuse them, explain them away.

What eloquent excuses we have: Times have changed!; I'm getting in touch with myself!; I need to try everything to find out who I am!; I'm no square!; I've got to look out for myself for a change!; My wife/husband doesn't understand me! On and on it goes—excuses, jokes, explanations to try to divert attention away from the fact that excuse-makers are not taking goodness seriously. They are only deluding themselves.

Next, there are the pollsters.

In answer to the "goodness" question, the pollsters conduct a survey to find out what the majority of people are doing, as if to suggest that numbers make it right. If everybody's doing it, then it must be all right—that is their motto. But we must realize that some things shouldn't be voted on. Sometimes the crowd is wrong! Sometimes we, in the name of goodness, must say No to the crowd. Sometimes we, in the name of goodness, must march to the beat of a different drummer. Sometimes, in the name of goodness, we must stand virtually alone, as did Moses and Joseph and Jeremiah and Jesus. But we are not alone! God is with us!

Then there are the legalists.

In answer to the question, "What does it mean to be good?" the legalists make laws; they try to legislate morality. They tell us what we can and cannot do. The problem is that legalism leads to a religion that is narrow, negative, burdensome, shallow, and filled with dread. Robert McAfee Brown, in *The Bible Speaks to You,* lists five objections to such legalism:

Objection One: Legalism forgets that religion is an active relationship with God in love. It reduces religion to "keeping-the-rules-so-I-won't-get-caught." It makes outward behavior more important than inner attitude. . . .

Objection Two: Legalism misunderstands the nature of God's love. It makes God's love something you have to earn by keeping the rules, whereas the whole claim of the New Testament is that God's love cannot be earned; it is a free gift. . . .

Objection Three: Legalism shifts the center of religious concern from God to man. Your number one concern becomes saving your own skin [by keeping the laws]. . . .

Objection Four: Legalism makes the individual proud. You are likely to start thinking: Say, I'm really doing pretty well. Broke only four rules today, out of 613, and that's batting well in any league. . . . This is the danger that always threatens the lives of "religious" people—the danger of smugness, or self-satisfaction. . . .

Objection Five: . . . Legalism has no power. It may tell you what is demanded of you, but it doesn't give you the power to fulfill the demands.

So if excuses won't work, and polls won't work, and laws won't work, what then is the answer? What does it mean to be good?

The New Testament answer:
There is no goodness apart from love!

There is only one norm which serves as the basis and foundation of goodness. That norm is *unselfish love.* Love sums up all the codes and all the ethical systems. Love contains within itself the essence of goodness. Although something I do may seem good, it is not good unless it is motivated by love.

Read the Sermon on the Mount. What is goodness there?—humble and unselfish love. Read the parables of

Jesus. What is goodness there?—seeking, forgiving, uncon-ditional love. Look at the cross. What is goodness there?—sacrificial, gracious, merciful love. You see, it is not enough to make excuses or conduct surveys or make laws. The only hope is love; the only answer is love; the only goodness is *love!*

Why Do Good People Suffer?

Why do good people suffer? This is the most difficult and challenging question that faces people of faith. It is the biggest hurdle, the most enormous obstacle that confronts our faith in a good and loving God. Just think of it:

- A hotel catches on fire, and scores of people are trapped and killed.
- A school bus slides off an icy road, and 34 children lose their lives.
- A news story tells of war in the Middle East; another, of bombings in London.
- A telephone call breaks the news you dreaded—your loved one has cancer.

The question that screams inside of us is Why? *Why* do these things happen? Why does God permit such things? Why does God allow war, disease, accidents, and sorrow? Why does God let good people suffer? Why did God let Jesus be nailed to a cross? Has God forsaken us?

Some years ago I was sitting in a hospital waiting room with a young woman who felt forsaken. The doctor had just brought the bad news about her husband.

In her anguish she cried out, "Doesn't God care? Why my husband? He has been a good man all his life. He has been honest and kind and loving. Now he has to die young, while people live on who have never done anything for anybody, have never been to church, have cheated and lied. Why? It's just not fair!" She buried her face in her hands.

Any person of faith must come to grips with the fact that these things do happen in God's world, making it difficult for many people to believe in God. Of course, I do not presume to know the full answer to the problem of human suffering. It is one of life's great mysteries. It is a problem so deep, so profound, so wrapped with holy awe, that from the beginning of time, people have pelted heaven with their prayers, asking, Why? The wisest of us cannot answer it completely, and yet somebody should say something in answer to that bothersome question, Why do good people suffer? I will try to bring some glimmer of light by sharing with you four insights I have gained from my struggle with the question.

First, people suffer because we live in a world governed by dependable natural laws.

"The rain falls on the just and on the unjust," is the way Jesus put it. The natural laws of the universe operate the same for all people. Take the law of gravity, for example. If a little child falls off the roof of a tall building, the law of gravity is merciless. Or think of a good man who is climbing a mountain. He is a devoted Christian, active in church and community. He loses his footing and falls a thousand feet to his death. The fact that he has an outstanding record in life makes no difference at all to the law of gravity. The law works for good and bad alike. There is no distinction. In this particular case, the law results in tragedy.

Cause and effect are bound together in dependable, unbending succession, and much of our suffering is a result of running head-on into these dependable laws of the universe. They make scientific advances possible, but when violated, they bring suffering. Yet we must have these dependable laws. They give order to creation, and without them, life would be complete chaos.

As Dr. J. S. Whale put it: "If water might suddenly freeze in midsummer; if the specific gravity of lead might at any time become that of thistledown; if pigs might fly or the White House turn into green cheese . . . man's life would be a nightmare."

Second, we suffer because we live in a world racked with growing pains.

There are so many things we don't know about our world, and what we don't know hurts us. We do things that bring suffering to ourselves and others, but we don't even realize it.

Just a little over a hundred years ago, we didn't know about germs. Before performing operations, surgeons would put on dirty overalls, like an auto mechanic. Doctors didn't bother to wash their hands before delivering a baby, and they had no idea that this had anything to do with the fact that so many babies and mothers died.

It makes you wonder, doesn't it? What will future generations say about us and the things we don't know or the things we are doing that unwittingly bring about our own suffering? Some of our suffering is a result of living in an unfinished world, a world racked with growing pains.

Third, we suffer because we live in a world of risky relationships.

God has made us so that we are not merely separate individuals, but a "family," woven together by loyalty, love, mutual need, and interdependence, into homes, friendships, communities, and nations. This fact of inescapable fellowship is the source of our greatest joys and our deepest hurts.

Almost every joy we know in life involves the element of risk. If I choose to love you, I am running the risk that you may reject me and break my heart—but love is worth the risk. People who have children, run the risk of heartache and sleepless nights—but children are worth the risk. The more deeply we love, the more deeply we can be hurt. Much suffering in our world today comes from risky relationships between persons, groups, and nations. Yet we would not forego the joys of love just because we are afraid of being hurt. It's worth the risk!

Fourth, we suffer because we live in a world that gives us freedom of choice.

God did not make us like puppets dangling from strings. God made us free, with freedom to choose our own way, and sometimes we make poor choices that bring suffering to ourselves and others.

A man decides that he can beat a train to a crossing and misses by only one second. A diplomat says the wrong thing, and two nations that have been allies for years find themselves at war. A teenage girl with a bright mind and a brilliant future becomes pregnant and drops out of school.

Our greatest gift in life is the gift of freedom of choice, but how we have misused it, and how we suffer from that ignorant or confused or wicked misuse of our free will!

One more thing can be said about suffering in our world, and this is the good news of our faith: We are not alone! God is with us, enabling us to suffer creatively. God never promised we would not suffer. God did promise to be with us, and God's presence enables us to turn our sorrows into triumphs and our defeats into victories.

Did Jesus Really Mean What He Said?

Dietrich Bonhoeffer, a German pastor and theologian, put it well when he said of Jesus, "In him, the message and the messenger became one!"

When we look at the Sermon on the Mount, we see, in a unique way, the mind of Jesus. When we read it, we remember that he not only taught it, he also lived it! He was the message and the messenger rolled into one.

Jesus *was* a peacemaker, he *was* humble-minded, he *was* merciful and genuine, he *did* hunger and thirst for righteousness, he *did* refuse to retaliate, or resent, or demand his rights. He *was* the salt of the earth, a light on a stand.

In this message and in this messenger, we see life as God meant it to be—real life! Sometimes I wonder with the song writer, "When will we ever learn?"

Dr. James Tucker Fisher was a pioneer in psychiatry. He studied under Freud and, for more than fifty years, specialized in psychosomatic medicine. At the close of his book *A Few Buttons Missing,* he wrote a powerful summary of a fascinating discovery:

> I dreamed of writing a handbook that would give a new and enlightened recipe for living a sane and meaningful life—a handbook that would be simple, practical, easy to understand and easy to follow. It would tell people how to live . . . what thoughts and attitudes and philosophies to cultivate and what pitfalls to avoid, in seeking mental health. I attended every symposium possible, took notes on the wise words of teachers and my colleagues who were leaders in the field . . . And then quite by accident, I discovered that such a work had already been completed, namely . . . the Sermon on the Mount. I now

believe this to be true: If you were to take the sum total of all the authoritative articles ever written by the most qualified of psychologists and psychiatrists on the subject of mental hygiene . . . if you were to combine them and refine them and cleave out all the excess verbiage . . . you would have an awkward and incomplete summation of the Sermon on the Mount. And it would suffer immeasurably through comparison.

The point is that for nearly two thousand years, we have held in our hands the key to life, the answer to the world's restless yearnings. Our problem is that we are not so sure we can trust it. Did Jesus really mean it? we ask. This business of:

- being meek
- turning the other cheek
- responding to evil with goodness
- loving the enemy
- going the second mile.

Did Jesus really mean that? we wonder.

Some years ago, a young professional baseball player prided himself on being a great hitter. He knew he could make it big in the majors if he just had a chance.

For several years he bounced around in the minor leagues, and then one year toward the end of the season, the major-league parent team brought him up. They were in the thick of a heated pennant race and needed help.

This was his chance! He was on a major league baseball team—a rookie, but nevertheless, a member of the team.

They promptly put him on the bench! Day after day went by, and the rookie was itching to bat, to show them what he could do.

Finally one day, the manager called for the rookie to pinch-hit. This was the dramatic moment he had dreamed of for so long—a crucial game, last inning, score tied, a runner on first base. This was his big moment! The rookie's heart pounded with excitement as he stepped into the batter's box.

Routinely, he glanced toward the third-base coach. He couldn't believe his eyes! He was given the signal to sacrifice! To sacrifice, the batter bunts—makes an out on purpose—to advance the runner to second base, in the hope that the next hitter can bring him in. The batter gives up his "life" at bat for the good of the team.

The rookie ignored the signal, took three hefty swings, and struck out. When he returned to the dug-out, he was met by an irate red-faced manager.

"Son, what's the matter with you? Didn't you see the signal to sacrifice?"

"Yes, Sir, I saw it," said the rookie, "but I didn't think you meant it!"

I saw it, but I didn't think you meant it! Isn't that what we say to God? On page after page of the Scriptures, God says to us, "Sacrifice! Sacrifice! Love others! Lay down your life for others! Sacrifice yourself for the good of the team! Lose yourself! Be self-giving!"

That is God's signal to us, but we are not so sure God means it. Well, Jesus showed us that God means it—he showed us on a cross!

How Does Faith Mend a Broken Heart?

Sooner or later, heartache comes to all of us. Sooner or later, one way or another, all our hearts are broken. Sadness, sorrow, disappointment, mourning, grief—whatever you wish to call it—rears its head and covers us like a heavy blanket. The "broken" heart is a fact of life. We need help in knowing how to deal with it, how to work through it, how to grow with it.

What does faith say to us about the grief experience? How does faith help mend a broken heart? Indeed, some special resources in the Christian faith will help bring healing to the hurt heart. Let me suggest a few that can serve us well as we walk through the dark valley of sorrow.

First, claim the fellowship of the church.

Let the church family's arms of love surround you and support you. Let the prayers, the tender expressions of concern, the gentle hugs, and warm words of assurance be means of strength for you. And never forget that no matter how alone you may feel in your heartache, you are not alone. God is with you! Nothing, not even death, can separate you from the love of God. So, let the worship and fellowship of the church surround you and uphold you. No matter how hurt you may feel, no matter how painful the experience, take part in the life of the church. Let the church be an integral part of the healing process.

Second, claim the power of helping others, which comes only from having gone through the grief pilgrimage.

Those who have gone through sorrow have a new empathy, a new sensitivity, a new compassion, a new power to help others.

Jesus said, "Blessed are those who mourn, for they shall be comforted!" The word *comforted* comes from two Latin words—*cum*, which means "with," and *fortis*, which means "strength." So the word *comforted* means literally "with strength"! Thus Jesus was saying, "Blessed are those who have gone through sorrow, for they are with strength."

Someone once put it like this: "Whoever among us has, through personal experience, learned what pain and anxiety are . . . belongs no more to himself alone; he is the brother of all who suffer."

Therefore, claim that strength to help others which comes only on the other side of trouble, only from walking through the valley of grief.

Last of all, claim the presence of God.

The "good news" of our faith is that God is with us in every circumstance of life and, indeed, beyond this life. Early in Matthew's Gospel, when he is trying to capture in words the meaning of Jesus, he uses the word *Emmanuel*, which means "God with us." The most important thing Jesus Christ shows us is *Emmanuel*, meaning that God is with us!

Again, in Romans 8, the apostle Paul underscores this important truth by reminding us that we are more than conquerors through the One who loved us because nothing, not even death, can separate us from God's love. In Par Lagervist's novel *Barabbas,* there is a poignant conversation between a Roman governor and one of his slaves, a Christian named Sahak, which makes the point boldly. The Roman speaks first:

- If you renounce your faith, no harm shall come to you. Will you do it?
- I cannot.
- Why not?
- I cannot deny my God.
- Extraordinary man . . . surely you must be aware of the punishment you force me to sentence you to. Are you really so brave that you can die for your faith?

- That is not for me to decide.
- Is not life dear to you?
- Yes. It is.
- But, if you do not forswear this God of yours, nothing can save you. You will lose your life.
- Yes, but I cannot lose the Lord my God! (p. 153)

That is the good news of our faith. We cannot lose the Lord our God. When we commit our lives to him, nothing can separate us from him and his love.

What Is the One Thing That Is Always Right?

Some years ago, I was teaching a course in religion at Lambuth College in Jackson, Tennessee. I was trying to help the students understand creative ways to approach the Scriptures and catch the excitement of the relevance of the Bible for our time and our lives. To make this vivid for them, one morning I divided the class into four groups—one in each corner of the room. I gave to each group a section of Paul's "love" chapter (I Cor. 13) and asked them to paraphrase it. "Read it . . . understand it . . . and then restate it in your own words," I told them.

When they had finished, we put their paraphrases together and came up with this modern version of I Corinthians 13, which they titled "Love Like Wow!":

Though I may be able to speak French, Spanish, and Japanese, and even rap with the angels, if I have not love, my speech is no more than a broken guitar or a scratched record.

I may preach like Billy Graham, have the brains of Einstein; I may have all the faith needed to put a Volkswagen into a phone booth, but if I have not love, I am nothing.

I may give the shirt off my back, and even smash my Steppenwolf albums (just to please my folks), but if I have not love, it does me no good.

Love is tolerant and tender;

Love is not stuck up or up-tight;

Love is not facetious, or snooty, or touchy;

Love is not pessimistic;

Love does not dig in the gutter or hunt for gossip, but rather is happy with the truth.

Love never cops out. . . . Its faith, hope, and patience never fail.

Love can outlast life (and the universe)!

People will talk forever, but never get things done. The Beatles may shake the world, but it is soon spent.

When perfect truth comes, life begins to take on meaning. And when love comes, the meaning of life is complete.

When I was a dumb kid, my whole life was wrapped up in immature selfishness and egotism, but now I have grown up and matured some, and I am embarrassed by and ashamed of vain self-centeredness.

Looking at life now is like looking in mirrors at the carnival. Things are twisted, distorted, fuzzy, but someday God will really open our eyes, and then we will be able to see life as God intended it.

Meanwhile, our survival kit must be supplied with faith, hope, and love.

Love is the greatest—so put love first!

Paul was right on target in his "love" chapter, and those students were pretty much on target in their contemporary paraphrase. Both have underscored the secret of real life—and the word is *love!* Love is the key to meaningful living; it is, indeed, the single most important thing in the world.

If we miss that—if we miss love—then we have missed life. Love is the one thing that is always right, always on target. If we fail in loving, then we fail altogether.

You see, you may have an educated mind, you may give your talents to worthwhile causes, you may rise to places of prominence in the eyes of other people, you may live an honorable and decent life. But even after you have done all those things, if you have left out love, you have missed the whole point of life. The absence of love is the reason many people today feel unhappy and restless. They feel empty and unfulfilled because they have not learned how to love.

Love is the one thing about which we can say, "If a person has this, that person's life is good." Without love, no matter what else we may have or do, our lives are failures. Love is the one thing that is always right. So as those college students said, "Put love first!"

Can Your Conscience Be Your Guide?

When we talk about religion, eventually we get around to the question of morality—the question of ethics. Right, wrong, good, bad—how do we tell the difference? The truth is that it is not always easy to make that distinction.

History illustrates this. Many of the people who put Jesus on the cross and the apostle Paul in prison honestly thought they were doing the right thing. Some of the worst things ever done in human history were done conscientiously, by people who honestly thought they were doing right. Remember the Crusades, the Inquisition, the Salem witch hunts, to name just a few. Bloody wars, cruel persecutions, shameful prejudices, brutal rituals, even human sacrifices—all have taken place in the name of "doing the right thing."

In our own time, we have been jolted by Jonestown . . . the events in Iran when 52 Americans were held hostage . . . and more recently, the events in the Persian Gulf, where the Iraqi military leaders aggressively invaded a defenseless nation, spewing out hostilities at the rest of the world—all in the name of religion.

People do become confused and perplexed when making ethical decisions. We are like the little boy who explained his report card with the comment, "But Mom, conduct is my hardest subject!"

"Let your conscience be your guide" is one answer often given to the moral dilemma. Well, can we? Can we simply follow our conscience when faced with questions of right and wrong? The answer is Yes and No! Yes, our conscience may help us, but our conscience also may be tricked or distorted or ignored. Some "distorted" consciences might be described as follows:

- *Worn-down Conscience.* If we do certain things enough, the conscience wears down, and these things don't seem wrong anymore.
- *Rationalized Conscience.* In the monumental novel *War and Peace,* the main character says it for us: "Yes, I have sinned, but I have several excellent excuses"!
- *Consequence Conscience.* This conscience worries only about getting caught.
- *Elastic Conscience.* This is the conscience that can be stretched to any compromise. Shakespeare spoke of a "conscience wide as hell."
- *Childish Conscience.* Here is the "naughty, naughty, mustn't do, or you will be punished" mindset. No significant commitments reside here, only the notion that religion is a neverending series of "thou shalt nots."

All these consciences are diseased. There is, however, a healthy and helpful *Mature Conscience*. It is ever-growing and established in positive commitments. The mature conscience does not trust feelings as much as it trusts the truth. The key to this conscience is that it is rooted in love, for there is no goodness apart from love, apart from active, loving goodwill toward all people. Love is the fixed point in a changing world! Unconditional, indiscriminate love is the measuring stick for the mature conscience.

Are There Different Pathways to God?

Dr. Roger Birkman, a psychologist in Houston, Texas, has developed a computer personality profile which suggests that, broadly speaking, there are four different personality styles:

First of all, there is the autocratic doer.

This person is action-oriented, or strong-willed. He or she means business and gets things done by taking charge and telling others exactly what to do.

Second, there is the detailed planner.

This person "plans his work, and then works his plan!" The detailed planner personality is precisely what the name implies—one who thinks things through in great detail and wants things done neatly, in order, and very systematically.

The third personality style
is the enthusiastic salesperson.

This person feels things strongly, is gregarious, outgoing, and emotionally charged. He or she comes on strong and wants others to plug in to that feeling level. Enthusiastic sales people are "people persons" and want others to experience what they are feeling; they want to "sell others" on their way, their style.

A fourth style is the artistic poetic philosopher.

This person is more soulful, more tuned in to beauty, reverence, awe. This personality is creative—one who enjoys quiet and pensive moments of solitude, who can tune in to the wonders of the universe and the mysteries of life.
Now, Birkman has an interesting way of clarifying these four personality styles so that we can recognize them more quickly and easily:

Imagine that you have nine cats in a house and that your task is to get the cats out of the house. How would you do it?
    The *autocratic doer* would take matters into his own hands. He would say "Scat!" and the cats had better get out if they know what's good for them. He means business and he is going to get this job done!
    The *detailed planner,* on the other hand, numbers the cats 1, 2, 3, 4, 5, 6, 7, 8, & 9, with nine neat signs, and then he puts nine neat holes in the wall and numbers them 1 through 9. Cat one must go out hole one; cat two must go out hole two; cat three must go out hole three . . . and if cat four runs out through hole 7, the detailed planner is completely frustrated! For him, it must be thought out systematically and worked out neatly!
    The *enthusiastic salesman,* excited by the challenge of his task, rises to the occasion. He opens all the doors and windows, gets some warm milk and cat food, goes outside, and

says, "Here Kitty, Kitty," and convinces the cats that they are better off outside anyway!

The *artistic poetic philosopher,* meanwhile, says "What in the world am I doing worrying about cats?"

Now, there are some important insights to grab hold of out of Birkman's personality profile. For one thing, it makes it clear that we are different! We are unique, and differentness is here to stay! We are different—different in appearance, in approach, in ideas, in tone, in emphasis. Some of us are action-oriented; some are pensive and thoughtful; some are loud; some are quiet; some are poetic; some are autocratic. Some plan, some sell, some think, and some do!

We *are* different! We have different personalities, temperaments, skills, priorities, gifts, attitudes, opinions, and styles. And that's OK—indeed, it is beautiful! It's OK to be different! As a matter of fact, God must love differentness and variety because he made so much of both.

The Scriptures speak of differentness as a necessary blessing: "Some are apostles, some prophets, some teachers," says the apostle Paul. "The body does not consist of one member but of many different members," and all are needed, all are helpful.

We are different, and it's all right to be different—as long as we are loving, kind, tolerant, respectful, and understanding about it.

But here is the rub: If we are insecure, then people who are different threaten us, and we can become scared and panicky and we react by trying to force our way on them. We want to make them to be like we are. We want to make them do it our way. We feel compelled to prove that our way is the right way, the valid way, the only way. And we may think the other person is cruel or stupid or insensitive.

But don't you see how wrong this is? Our religion is the response of our unique personality to the personality of God.

And since our individual personalities are different, our individual pathways to God are different.

Every person is a unique child of God! We must not miss that! We dare not take the uniqueness away!

What Is the Key Sign of Faith?

One of the highest compliments we can give someone is to call him or her a magnanimous person. Clarence Hall called *magnanimity* the "noblest of human graces." Magnanimity—what does it mean?

Well, it's a million-dollar word for a rich spirit. The dictionary defines *magnanimity* as the "quality of being big in spirit, gentle, kind, considerate, rising above pettiness or meanness, forgiving, gracious, and generous in overlooking injury or insult."

The apostle Paul, writing a long time ago to his friends at Philippi, called the spirit of magnanimity the essential spirit of the Christian. He told the Philippians that a Christian should be characterized by magnanimity and that this bigness of spirit should be obvious to others—not silent and secretive, but radiant and infectious, as bright as the sunlight and as loud as the rushing wind: "Let your magnanimity be manifest to all," said Paul (Phil. 4:5 NEB).

What is magnanimity? We see it in Abraham Lincoln. He was a big man, and a man big in spirit. He showed marvelous magnanimity, especially toward General McClellan, whom he appointed to command the armies of the North in the war between the states. McClellan was a brash young upstart, an obnoxious man. Yet because Lincoln respected and trusted McClellan as a soldier, he suffered his personal insults patiently.

One evening, President Lincoln and a colleague went to McClellan's home on a matter of great urgency concerning the war. Of course, people normally go to the President; but Lincoln, wanting not to inconvenience McClellan, went to his home. After keeping the men waiting for a while, McClellan sent word by a servant that he was just too tired to see the President. Lincoln's colleague was indignant; the other cabinet members wanted McClellan kicked out immediately for this insubordination and rudeness.

But Lincoln replied, "I will gladly hold General McClellan's stirrup for him, if he will only win us victories!" That's magnanimity!

Lincoln received insults also from other public figures. Edwin Stanton publicly denounced him as a fool, a low, cunning clown, and "the original gorilla." Do you know what the President did? He appointed Stanton Secretary of War because he thought Stanton was the best man for the job! That's magnanimity!

We see magnanimity in this famous poem by Edwin Markham:

> He drew a circle that shut me out—
> Heretic, rebel, a thing to flout.
> But Love and I had the wit to win:
> We drew a circle that took him in!

We see magnanimity in Booker T. Washington, the great African American educator. One day as Professor Washington was walking to work at Tuskegee Institute in Alabama, he happened to pass the mansion of a wealthy woman.

The woman, not recognizing him, called out, "Hey you! Come here! I need some wood chopped!"

Without a word, Dr. Washington peeled off his jacket, picked up the ax, and went to work. He not only cut a large pile of wood, he also carried the firewood into the house and arranged it neatly.

He had scarcely left when a servant said to the woman, "I guess you didn't recognize him, ma'am, but that was Professor Washington!" Embarrassed and ashamed, the woman hurried over to Tuskegee Institute to apologize.

Booker T. Washington replied: "There's no need to apologize, madam. I'm delighted to do favors for my friends!" That's magnanimity!

We also see magnanimity in this classic definition of a *saint*. Someone once asked, "What made the saints, saints?" and this was the answer given: "Because they were cheerful when it was difficult to be cheerful; patient when it was difficult to be patient; and because they pushed on when they wanted to stand still, kept silent when they wanted to talk, and were agreeable when they wanted to be disagreeable." That was all. It was quite simple, really, and it always will be. That's magnanimity!

Of course, we see the best portrait of magnanimity in Jesus Christ. He taught it in the Sermon on the Mount—"Go the second mile," he said. "Give up your cloak as well as your coat"; "Pray for those who persecute you"; "Be merciful, like your Father in heaven." That's magnanimity!

Jesus didn't just teach it and talk about it. He *lived* magnanimously! Think of . . .

- Jesus saying, "Let the children come," and then taking them up in his arms;
- Jesus saying to the woman taken in adultery, "Neither do I condemn you; go and sin no more";
- Jesus on the cross, praying, "Father, forgive them, for they know not what they do"!

That's magnanimity! It's a good word for our vocabularies and a great spirit for our lives.

Where Is Hope in This Desperate World?

We are living in desperate times, in a world that breeds cynicism and despair. Just think of it: homes robbed; people attacked and brutalized; frightening drug problems everywhere; the cost of living escalating; the dollar shrinking; and one international conflict after another. It's enough to make Norman Vincent Peale a pessimist!

In this kind of crazy, troubled world, we need to be careful, we need to be cautious, we need to be wary. But we dare not become paranoid; we dare not become somber cynics; we must not give in to a frightened, depressed pessimism. We must not lose hope!

The question is, How can we believe the best things in the worst times? How can we hold on to the miracle of hope? How can we keep trusting and hoping for the best in such strange, violent times?

Some years ago, a U.S. submarine sank off the coast of Massachusetts, becoming a prison for its crew. Ships were rushed to the scene to attempt a rescue. Divers went down to see if anything could be done. The men in the submarine clung desperately to life, waiting to be rescued. Slowly but surely, their oxygen supply was running out. The divers outside the sub and the frightened men inside communicated by tapping Morse code on the wall of the submarine. Time was running out and they knew it.

After a long pause, a question was slowly tapped out from inside the submarine: "Is . . . there . . . any . . . hope?"

And that is the question every one of us must ask and answer at some point in life. Many are asking it now.

In his novel *Don Quixote,* Cervantes answers the question for us by saying, "While there's life there's hope!" The great people of faith have always believed that; they have always been people of hope:

- Moses, caught between Pharaoh's army and the Red Sea—a seemingly hopeless situation—went forward and trusted God to open a way.

- Shadrach, Meshach, and Abednego went into the fiery furnace—into a seemingly hopeless situation. They trusted God to be with them, and he was.

- David stood before Goliath. What chance could a little boy with a slingshot have against this giant of a warrior? But David believed that God was with him, and it made all the difference.

- The apostle Paul was a master in the art of hopeful living. He knew how to handle opposing circumstances, how to overcome handicaps, how to turn the hard situations of life into good. Toward the end of his life, he was arrested and put in prison. He was separated from his friends, cut off from his dream of going to Spain; he was sick and faced death. Talk about a hopeless situation! Who would have blamed Paul if he had given up? But he refused to give in to self-pity. He refused to give in to disillusionment. He refused to give in to bitterness. He refused to quit. He kept on believing, trusting, hoping.

And remember Jesus. He taught hope. He lived it. He died for it. Just think of it. They betrayed him, mocked him, beat him, taunted him, spat on him, and nailed him to a cross, but he kept on believing in people and in his Father. Jesus knew as much about the hard knocks of life as the cynics know. He knew that people could be cruel. He knew that life could be unfair. But he never gave up on people, he never quit on life, he never ran out on God.

Jesus, in his life and teachings and death, calls us to be people of hope, people who believe the best things in the worst times, people who hang on to the miracle of hope in a desperate world.

Who in the World Wants to Be a Saint?

Who would want to be a saint these days, in this kind of world? Why, the very word conjures up all sorts of unreal people—people in stained-glass windows or on pages of Scripture, or at least people who have been dead for many years. Today, we use the word *saint* occasionally to describe a pious person—but the kind we don't want to be, the kind we subtly denounce and quickly disassociate ourselves from, by saying rather dramatically, "I'm no saint!"

Will Rogers saw it pretty clearly, and he cut right to the heart of it. Commenting on his visit to Rome, he said he found it interesting that "everybody wants to see where St. Peter was buried, but no one wants to live like him." I guess we all could afford to think about that a bit, couldn't we?

Actually, the word *saint* is a good word gone wrong. The apostle Paul used it frequently and evidently gave it a completely different meaning. In fact, he didn't use *saint* to refer to pious, sanctimonious, puritanical people at all. If you study his letters in the New Testament closely, you will notice that he writes to the "saints" in Rome, Corinth, Ephesus, and Philippi, and there was nothing unreal or pietistic about those people! And they were very much alive, sometimes a little more lively than Paul wanted them to be. As a matter of fact, sometimes after he called these people saints, he proceeded to scold them for "unsaintly behaviour."

Now, what are we to make of this? Are we called to be saints? Now? In this world? The answer is Yes! The biblical answer is Absolutely! But we need to reclaim the word, redefine it, reunderstand it. As the old saying goes, you can call me anything if you let me define the terms!

So let me define the term. Let me tell you what I think a true saint is. This is not a textbook answer or a dictionary definition, but an answer out of my own personal experience with people I believe were saints in the best sense of the word, people who exhibited the following characteristics:

A saint makes goodness attractive.

Somehow, over the years, we have twisted it around. A genuine saint is not a person who turns you off spiritually, but just the opposite—one who makes goodness so attractive, so appealing, that when you are with that person, you find yourself challenged, feeling that "I wish I could be more like that!"

A saint makes it easy for others to believe in God.

The best argument for faith is a person who really lives it. How powerfully we see this in Jesus and the impact of his influence. Because of him, the weak and vascillating Simon Peter became a "rock"; a woman of the streets, Mary Magdalene, became a woman of faith; the self-seeking James became one who gave everything, even his life. The real measure of Jesus is not just what he did, but what others did, and are doing, because of him.

A saint believes the best things during the worst times.

A saint is one who is spiritually tenacious, who keeps on believing when it's difficult to believe. It is Job, in great pain, crying, "Though he slay me, yet will I trust him!" It is Bonhoeffer, praying in a concentration camp, "Lord whatever this day may bring . . . Thy name be praised!"

A saint does ordinary things in extraordinary ways.

I was thinking recently of a man who influenced my life and the lives of many young people. He was a youth counselor in my home church. He couldn't preach a sermon; he couldn't carry a tune in a bucket; he couldn't teach a class publicly, for he was shy. But he was genuine, and you knew it immediately. He loved God and the church, and he really cared for young people. He made terrific hamburgers. Every Sunday night he was at the church cooking hamburgers—an ordinary thing, but he did it in an extraordinary "saintly" way, and God's work prospered because of him.

A saint loves even the unlovable.

Loving the outcast, loving the "shut-out," loving those who don't love you back, loving those nobody else seems to care for—nothing is more saintly than that.

Can You Choose Your Own Attitudes?

Madeline Hildreth, one of the outstanding book reviewers in the nation, is an inspiration to many—not only because of her talent as a reviewer, but because of her inner strength, her determination, and the great attitudes that have helped her overcome a terrific hurdle, polio. Here are her words:

When I was three years old, I was one of the first nine people to have the disease diagnosed as poliomyelitis in New York state; and I was nearly sixteen before a series of long hospital stays and endless operations enabled me to put my feet on the floor and, with the aid of heavy braces and crutches, begin to walk. I've never been able to walk across an open field or play a game of tennis or go to a dance. I know the meaning of frustration. I've had to work hard on my attitudes. I couldn't permit myself to be eaten out by the virus of self-pity, or jealousy for those who, without any effort, possessed something that I have worked my head off to gain and will never have. I have lived in a prison cell, in a body I could not control. What am I to do? The Christian answer is to move forward. If life gives us a lemon, then we must make it into a refreshing lemonade.

That's just what she has done, and she has done it with a great Christian attitude. Attitude is so important in life. We can't emphasize that too much! The great coach Vince Lombardi once pointed out that football is 75 percent attitude. The same thing could be said about life—it's 75 percent attitude. You and I are what we are because of our attitudes. Attitude is the difference between defeat and victory, despair and hope, sadness and joy. Our lives are determined by attitude. If you change your attitudes, you can change your life.

The writer of Proverbs said it like this: "As a man thinks in his heart so is he" (Prov. 23:7 KJV). In other words, whatever gets hold of you in your innermost being is the thing that controls your life. Whatever we think about, dwell upon, give ourselves to, is what controls our lives.

Jesus realized this when he said, "Seek first the kingdom of God and everything else will be taken care of." The apostle Paul expressed it like this: "I appeal to you brethren—to present your bodies as a living sacrifice, holy, committed to God"—that is, give everything, even your attitudes, completely to God.

One of the most fascinating books I have read is Viktor Frankl's *Man's Search for Meaning*. For years, Dr. Frankl, an Austrian psychiatrist, was a prisoner in German concentration camps. During that time, he noticed that some prisoners, although they looked physically robust, were actually weak because of their attitudes. Others, those who had positive attitudes, were much stronger and an inspiration to all in the camp. Frankl writes:

> We who lived in concentration camps can remember the men who walked through the huts comforting others, giving away their last piece of bread. They may have been few in number, but they offer sufficient proof that everything can be taken from a man but one thing: the last of the human freedoms—to choose one's attitude in any given set of circumstances, to choose one's way.

Paul said, "Don't let the world around you squeeze you into its mold" (Rom. 12:2 Phillips). The world around us doesn't determine what we are. Circumstances do not make us. It is our attitudes that determine who we are and what kind of world we really live in. Captain Eddie Rickenbacker once wrote these words:

If you think about disaster you will get it. Brood about death and you will hasten your demise. Think positively and masterfully, with confidence and faith, and life becomes more secure, more fraught with action, richer in achievement and experience. (T. Cecil Myers, *Living on Tiptoe,* p. 64)

You can change your attitudes and thus change your life! You see, your destiny is not a matter of chance. It is a matter of choice. Each of us chooses our own destiny by choosing our attitudes toward life.

What Was Special About Jesus?

The Roman centurion saw it; he saw the truth as he stood at the foot of the cross. Jesus had just breathed his last, and as the Roman looked up at the Nazarene, his mind replayed the dramatic events that had taken place so quickly during the last few days.

- He had seen Jesus riding into Jerusalem on a donkey, palm branches strewn before him—recognized as a king and yet not interested in earthly kingdoms.
- He had heard Jesus teaching with keen insight and authority in public places.
- He had seen Jesus arrested, accused, convicted, mocked, jeered, slapped, and spat upon.
- He had seen Jesus brutally crucified, and had noticed that he didn't struggle.

- He had heard Jesus pray that his executioners be forgiven.
- He had seen Jesus console the thief on the adjacent cross.
- He had seen Jesus make provisions for the care of his mother, even as he was in anguish.
- And finally, the Roman centurion had seen Jesus of Nazareth die.

As he looked up at Jesus, the Centurion said it for all of us: "Truly, this man was the Son of God!" Could it be that this was his way of saying that this man was so good, so authentic, so genuine that he must be *true?*

Jesus was God's Son, God's word become flesh, God's idea "lived out." He was *true* to what God meant life to be. Isn't it interesting that even in his death, Jesus showed us how to live? Even as he died, he revealed the most authentic qualities of life. A few of these qualities emerge so graphically from the cross that they must be true, they must be of God.

First, Jesus showed us love.

Love is so good, so beautiful, so fulfilling, so right, that it must be true. Jesus believed that. He went to the cross for it. Love is so special that it must be true to life as God meant it to be. Recently, I saw our daughter do something thoughtful for her brother. That simple act of kindness made me feel great joy, and I thought, "As parents, there is nothing that makes us happier than to see our children love each other, help each other, care for each other." Of course, sometimes they annoy each other, and that always bothers us.

That's a parable for life, isn't it? I'm sure nothing makes God happier than to see us love one another. I'm equally sure that when we hurt one another, it breaks God's heart, because God made us out of love and for love. Love is so good that it must be true life as God meant it to be. If you doubt that, consider the alternatives—hate, cruelty, hostility, indifference. No, those are all false, distortions of God's plan and God's truth. The truth is that God made us for love.

Second, Jesus showed us humility.

There is something very special, very God-like, about the spirit of humility. A Christian leader visiting in China asked a group of Chinese pastors what it was in Christ that appealed most to them and won their hearts. Nobody mentioned the miracles or even the Sermon on the Mount. One of the elders, in a choking, faltering voice, told the story of the upper room, when Christ washed the disciples' feet. He became a humble servant. Humility is so good that it must be life as God meant it to be. If you doubt that, consider the alternatives—pompous pride, self-centered arrogance, egotistical acts. No, all of those are false, distortions of God's will for our lives. The truth is that God made us for love and humility.

Third, Jesus showed us forgiveness.

Forgiveness is another quality, or spirit, that is so special it must be true. Hear Jesus on the cross, saying, "Father, forgive them!" That is so good it must be authentic, it must be of God. So if you ever wonder, "Should I forgive that person who has wronged me or hurt me?" just remember Jesus on a cross, saying, "Father, forgive them." That is our measuring stick for forgiveness. That is the way God wants us to be. If you doubt that, consider the alternatives—resentment, bitterness, vengeance. No, all those are false, distortions of God's will for our lives. The truth is that God made us for love, humility, and forgiveness. Jesus showed us that on a cross! He died that we might live. He rose again to show us that love, humility, and forgiveness cannot be killed. They are of God, and they are eternal.

How Do You Develop a Strong Faith?

Some years ago—perhaps I should say *many* years ago—I was a basketball player. I went to college on an athletic scholarship in the "old days," when a college athlete participated in more than one sport; I played basketball and baseball and ran track. At the time, I was in excellent physical condition and a pretty fair athlete.

However, a short time ago, I embarrassed myself silly in a basketball game. A group of ministers were asked to play a fifteen-minute basketball game, just prior to a regular intercollegiate varsity game. I played in that preliminary game! This is what happened:

- My mind said, "Intercept that pass! Dribble full-speed down the court, fake out the defender, dribble behind your back, then soar up for a crowd-pleasing, swooping, double-pump reverse left-hand lay-up!" Now, that's what my mind said to my body.
- My body answered, "Who, me?"
- My mind said: "Yes, you! You can do it! You have done it before, and you can do it now—go to it!" That's what my mind said to my body.
- My body answered, "You've gotta be kidding!"

You see, my body refused to respond because it had been a long time since it had been used in that way. I hadn't exercised, I hadn't practiced, I hadn't played—it was awful!

I was so bad that I was the third most embarrassed person in that arena. The two most embarrassed were our children, who kept saying over and over, "Just think. After this is over, he is actually gonna come up here and sit beside us!"

That Saturday afternoon, I learned the agonizing truth of a basic principle: "If you don't use it, you lose it." As I learned the hard way, this is true in athletics. It is true in music. It is true intellectually. But nowhere is it more true than on the spiritual level.

If you want a good strong faith, what do you do? You practice, you work at it. If you want a meaningful prayer life, what do you do? You pray—you pray a lot. If you want a good understanding of the Bible, what do you do? You study and study the Scriptures—and then you study some more.

That's the choice open to us spiritually, isn't it? We must use it or we lose it!

How Does Faith Free You from Paralyzing Fear?

Recently I ran across some rather poignant words evidently written by a teenager who longed to touch the world and taste life, but was afraid of the risks, the demands, the responsibilities. I have included a few words of the poem here, and though I don't know its author, I hope that young person overcame the fear and lived a happy, useful life.

> I want to touch you, world,
> but I don't want to leave my shell.

Does that sound familiar to you? It does to me. It reminds me of something I have felt before. It also reminds me of something in the Bible—Jesus' parable of the talents in the Gospel of Matthew.

There Jesus told about a man who was about to make a trip

to a far country. Just before leaving, he called in three servants and gave them oversight of his money. To one, he gave five talents; to another, two talents, and to the last, he gave one talent. Then he left on his journey. While he was gone, the first two servants doubled their talents, but the one-talent servant dug a hole in the ground and hid his master's money because he was afraid he might lose it. When the master returned, he was much displeased with the one-talent servant.

What went wrong? Why did the one-talent servant fail? Well, he failed because he did nothing! He did nothing because he was *afraid!* He was paralyzed by his own fears! Consider the fears that caused him to freeze and fail, see if you find yourself somewhere between these lines.

First, he was afraid of a new challenge.

He was afraid of a new idea. As the master rode off into the sunset, can't you just hear the one-talent servant muttering, "We never did it that way before!" This, of course, is the sin of the closed mind, and nothing is more paralyzing than closed-mindedness.

Second, he was afraid he might not do as well as the others.

He was afraid he wouldn't measure up, that his pride would be wounded. He was afraid of loss of face. So he refused to play the game. Like a child, he tried to cover his fear by not participating.

Third, he was afraid of work.

His master called him "slothful," lazy. But I think it runs deeper than plain old laziness. The real tragedy of the one-talent servant is not that he buried his gift and made no money. The real tragedy is that he had no purpose! People with a purpose are never lazy. Their work becomes an exciting expression of their purpose and faith.

Fourth, he was afraid of his master.

He said, "I knew you to be a hard man, and I was afraid." One of the most important things Jesus shows us is that God is a loving parent. So we don't need to run scared. We don't need to be afraid of our master.

Fifth, he was afraid to act.

He failed because he did nothing! I heard of a man who went to see his doctor. After the check-up, the doctor told him, "The best thing you can do is stop drinking, go on a diet, start jogging, and stop carousing around town at all hours."

The man was thoughtful for a moment; then he asked, *"What's the next best thing?"*

Isn't that the way many of us are? We feel ourselves getting caught in a trap and we want to break free, but we are afraid to pay the price, afraid to act—and we do nothing, trapped in a prison of fear.

How do we get out of that prison? How do we get over these paralyzing fears? Well, the answer is simple. Love is the freeing agent. Love casts out fear.

In Marburg, Germany, some years ago, something happened that illustrates the power of love to set us free. A mother had taken her young daughter to the circus. All of a sudden, the child slipped away from her mother and disappeared. Picture the mother's horror when she saw that the child had somehow squeezed through the bars of the lion's cage and was standing just a few feet from a ferocious lion. The mother, without hesitation, ran into the cage, grabbed the child in her arms, brought her out of the cage, and slammed the door in the face of the pursuing lion. And then she promptly fainted!

Now, that woman feared that lion as much as you and I would. But she is a mother! And her love for her endangered child cast out any sense of fear she might have had and sent her to do something—a risky, dangerous something—she would have thought impossible for her to do.

The point is clear: Love is the freeing agent. When love is strong enough, it casts out fear and brings us out of whatever imprisons us. Love sets us free to be God's children—God's stewards in this world.

Do You Need Other People?

Let me begin with a riddle: Why is the Robinson Crusoe story a possibility, but the Tarzan story is an impossibility?

Both men were lost in wilderness places—one on a deserted island, the other in a dense jungle. But only the Robinson Crusoe story is acceptable to the thoughtful student.

The Robinson Crusoe story is possible because Crusoe was an adult whose personality was already formed when he was washed up on the island. Besides, he had a companion, Friday, a person to whom he could relate.

On the other hand, the Tarzan story is an impossibility because, according to the comic-book story, Tarzan was lost in the jungle as a tiny infant. As a small baby, he survived the plane crash and was adopted and reared by apes. Now, sociological studies have shown this to be quite impossible. If baby Tarzan had survived, he would never have acted like a human being, but like an ape. He would have thought he was an ape!

The classic documentation of this fact is the famous "wolf children" sociological study. Two human infants were adopted by wolves. When discovered, the children had been with the wolves for some time. The sociologists who found them named them for the mythological Romulus and Remus. After observing them in a laboratory setting, the sociologists realized that Romulus and Remus had no understanding of their human personhood. They thought they were wolves, and they played the part to perfection. They walked on all fours, they snarled and howled, and when a live chicken was put in the room with them, they attacked it, ripped it apart, and devoured it. A short time after being brought to civilization, the wolf children died—apparently lonely for the wolf pack, lonely for what they thought was their native environment.

This reminds us of the importance of our relationships. We are relational people. We are what we are because of our relationships. The old saying—Mind the company you keep!—emphasizes the idea that we tend to become like those with whom we associate. If you change my relationships, you change me; you change my life.

Our relationships are tremendously important because we were made for community. God made us to live together. Someone has said that the deepest need of people is a sense of community, a sense of acceptance and belonging, of being "at one" with other persons.

A lonely little boy wishing for some playmates once said to his mother, "Mom, I wish I were two little puppies, so I could play together." That childish remark is theologically and psychologically profound. An old Latin proverb put it like this: One man is no man at all. We were made for community.

Robert McAfee Brown, in *The Significance of the Church,*

suggests something that at first sounds shocking—that the modern cocktail party is the distorted and secularized longing of people for the Lord's Supper; that deep down inside, people are longing frantically for Holy Communion, for oneness, for acceptance, for belonging.

If you think about it, even our language is our persistent endeavor to escape from solitariness, to discover a world of companions, to create a device of communication in order to have friends. We need friends so that we can think together, speak together, play together, plan together, and build a community together. This instinct for community is deep-seated within us, for God planted it there and wants us to share life together.

One of our greatest temptations is to forget that. The temptation is to say "I" rather than "we," "mine" rather than "ours," "me" rather than "us." Karle Baker expresses it well in his poem "Pronouns":

The Lord said,
"Say, 'We' ";
But I shook my head,
Hid my hands tight behind my back, and said,
Stubbornly,
"I."

The Lord said,
"Say, 'We' ";
But I looked upon them, grimy and all awry.
Myself in all those twisted shapes?
Ah, no!
Distastefully I turned my head away,
Persisting,
"They."

The Lord said,
"Say, 'We' ";
And I
At last,

Richer by a hoard
Of years
And tears,
Looked in their eyes and found the heavy word
That bent my neck and bowed my head:
Like a shamed schoolboy then I mumbled low,
"We,
Lord."

Why Is a Good Start Not Enough?

The telephone rang loudly in a police station in New York City. The sergeant at the precinct desk handled the call with dispatch. He knew exactly what to do, because he had handled this kind of call many times before. It was routine now—almost commonplace. Another drunk was lying in a street gutter in the Bowery.

Quickly, the police and the emergency squad were on the scene, sirens blaring, lights flashing. They did their best to revive the man, but it was too late. He had breathed his last.

Some of the on-lookers who were familiar with the people and the happenings in the Bowery recognized the dead man in the gutter. He was a well-known character who went about selling shoestrings and cigarette butts for drinks. He was in his late forties, but he looked at least seventy because of the kind of life he had been leading. In a sense, he had unconsciously committed suicide—drowning himself in a relentless sea of alcoholic drinks. Another Bowery drunk had died.

"What's so unusual about that? It's a common enough occurrence," you may say. Some of you may have been to New

York City and may have seen first-hand the heart-breaking sights—men and women begging for drinks, or lying unconscious on sidewalks and in gutters, or sleeping in alleys and deserted storefronts with only rumpled newspapers for cover.

That's what the police found that day—another man who had literally drunk himself to death. However, when they reached the city morgue with the body there was something unusual: They found not only his identification papers, but in his pocket they found a Phi Beta Kappa key. Further investigation revealed that he had been brought up in a fine home and had graduated from Harvard University with a perfect four-point academic record.

What had happened? Wouldn't you like to know the rest of that story? I'm sorry I don't know more. However, out of what we do know of the story, one thing is clear: Though that man died that day in the Bowery, he had quit on life a long time before that moment of physical death.

Sadly, far too many people—like the man in the Bowery, although less dramatically than he—give in to the desire to quit on life. They start out well, with starry eyes, great fervor, ready to conquer the world and live life to the full; but then come problems, difficulties, nuisances, burdens, troubles, disappointments, heartaches.

Suddenly, they feel hoodwinked and deceived, and they are ready to throw in the towel and give up. Then life is merely a series of escapes. No longer do they really live. They vegetate, they endure, they exist, they get by, they make it through the day—but in essence they have quit on life.

Don't let that happen to you! Don't shrink back or give up! Our calling as people of faith is to move forward and celebrate life!

How Does Faith Bring Serenity?

One of the most impressive aspects of Holy Week is the serenity of Jesus in those difficult hours and days that led to the cross. His strength of character is nothing short of amazing! His deep sense of peace, his quiet confidence, his inner calm, his courage, his serenity of spirit—whatever you want to call that quality of poise and composure—stands out vividly!

We see that serenity even more dramatically as the Gospel writers set it alongside the nervous personality of Pontius Pilate. Telescope in on that scene with me—Jesus standing on trial before the Roman governor Pilate. What a contrast! How different these two men are!

Now, if you asked someone who knew nothing of the story to point out the "strong" person in this scene, using our present-day standards, the person would point quickly to Pilate, and would document that choice by underscoring Pilate's wealth, position, power, authority, political clout, and fame. And yet, that choice would be wrong—so very wrong!

Who has the inner peace and real strength here? Not Pilate! Pilate has the outer strength, but not the inner stability. It's obvious, as you look more closely, that Jesus is the strong one here. In fact, his inner strength and serenity completely baffle Pilate.

First, look at Pilate.

He is confused, upset, weak. He can't make up his mind. In a dither, he runs from one group to another asking questions here and there. He tries to pass the buck to Herod. Pilate knows that Jesus is innocent, but he does not have the strength of character to stand firm for what is right. This is a picture of a man running scared. Outwardly, the Roman governor has it all—power, wealth, position, fame—but inwardly, where it really counts, he is scared to death, nervous as a long-tailed cat in a room full of rocking chairs!

Finally, Pilate washes his hands, trying to straddle the fence. Like a nervous politician, he gives the people what they want—he turns Jesus over to them for execution. But just in case someone else may see it differently, he tries to act as if he is not really involved.

Now, is that strength of character? Is that peace of mind? Is that serenity of spirit? Is being scared, confused, and weak the picture of strength? Surely not!

On the other hand, look at Jesus.

He stands poised, confident, unafraid, serene. He is facing death, but his strength never wavers. Just think of it:

- an unfair trial for an innocent man,
- lies, plotting, conniving,
- bribed witnesses, political intrigue,
- jealousy, hostility, hatred,
- a mob scene, and a kangaroo court.

And in the face of it all, Jesus exhibits an incredible quality of inner peace, strength, and calm. They betray him, deny him, taunt him, beat him, curse him, spit upon him, and nail him to a cross. But he says, "Father, forgive them, they know not what they do"! That is strength of character, isn't it? That is inner peace and spiritual maturity.

Now, the question is this: What produced that amazing strength of character and moral fiber in Jesus?

- He knew who he was!
- He knew where he was going!
- He knew Who was with him!

What Are the Qualities of Spiritual Maturity?

An eminent psychiatrist, G. B. Chisholm, once made a significant and provocative statement that gives us something to think about: "So far in the history of the world, there have never been enough mature people in the right places." That is a real problem, isn't it? We settle for childishness, rather than pay the price for maturity. Just think about it.

- In politics, how childish we have become! A candidate promises "mature leadership" and then spends the entire campaign attacking the opponent with ugly smear tactics. They never get around to the real issues. In a recent local election, I voted on every race but one. I could not bring myself to vote for either candidate, because I felt that both had been so embarrassingly childish.
- What about international affairs? One nation says to another, "If you don't do what I want, then I won't talk to you anymore!"
- And how about entertainment? You are driving along, when suddenly over the car radio comes a smooth, suave

voice telling you about a new form of entertainment that has come to town. "It is not for everybody," the voice assures you. It is mature, sophisticated, thought-provoking, designed for intelligent audiences. You are interested, until you realize that the announcer is plugging a new movie, *Sex Kittens on College Campus*!

Jesus saw the dangers and problems connected with this kind of childish immaturity. Much of his teaching has this meaning: "Grow up! Don't act like spoiled children! Be mature!" With this in mind, let me quickly outline some characteristics of spiritually mature people.

First, spiritually mature people know how to handle frustration.

They know how to deal with disappointment, how to turn problems into opportunities and defeats into victories. If a child does not get the toy it wants, the child may scream, cry, throw something, scratch or bite or hit. Put that kind of immature response to frustration on a bigger stage, and it can be devastating. It makes you wonder how many lives have been lost, wars started, families alienated, marriages destroyed, communities disrupted, persons hurt, because of childish, immature people who have not learned how to handle frustration.

Second, spiritually mature people know how to take responsibility for their own lives.

Childish people expect special favors. They want somebody else to "do it for them," and they blame others when things don't go their way. Childish people ask, What's in it for me? Mature people take charge of their own lives.

Third, spiritually mature people
know how to forgive.

Childish people want to get even. Mature people want to forgive! If you ever wonder, "Should I forgive that person who has hurt me or wronged me?" remember the picture of Jesus hanging on the cross, saying, "Father, forgive them." That is our measuring stick for forgiveness and maturity.

Fourth, spiritually mature people
know how to be self-giving.

Childish people are selfish. Mature people are loving. A paraphrase of the apostle Paul's words in the love chapter says it all: "Put away childish things. Grow up and learn how to love. The greatest of these, the most mature of these, is love" (I Cor. 13).

Why Not You?

Scott Levy, a pastor in the Midwest, was preaching for a pastor friend one Sunday morning. He went early to the church to see what it was like and get the feel of the atmosphere.

As he was walking down a long hallway, his sermon notes in one hand and his pulpit robe draped over the other arm, he came upon a large room used as a nursery for preschoolers. Glancing in, he saw a little boy who looked about four years old, sitting all by himself.

The little boy said, "Hi, my name's Tommy, and I'm all alone in this big room."

Scott, who had done a lot of counseling, decided to use his nondirective counseling technique on the little boy.

He answered back, "You feel all alone in that room?"

"I don't just feel it," said the little boy. "I *know* I am all alone!"

Trying to reassure the boy, Scott replied confidently, "Don't you worry now. I'm sure that before too long somebody will come to be with you."

With wistful eyes, little Tommy looked up at him and said, *"Why not you?"*

Why not you? That question resounds across the ages, and yet, more often than not, we ignore it, neglect it, fail to hear it, or refuse to act upon it. More often than not, we hope that someone else will come along and do what needs to be done.

- A problem needs to be solved.
- A word needs to be spoken.
- A job needs to be done.
- A situation needs to be corrected.
- A person needs to be helped.
- A church needs to be reformed.
- A community needs to be improved.
- A reconciliation needs to be worked out.
- A word of appreciation needs to be expressed.
- A wrong needs to be righted.

We know it. We see it. We want these things done, but we expect somebody else to see to it. We feel that someone else more talented or more eloquent or more authoritative or more committed will come along and do what needs to be done.

But the question that God has directed to each one of us is simply this: "Why not you?" One of the most significant keys to successful and meaningful living is found in being able to see something that should be done and then doing something about it.

When you stop to think about it, you can see that the great people of faith in the Scriptures and down through the pages of history were people who saw a situation that needed to be made better, people who heard the call of God in that penetrating personal question, "Why not you? Why don't *you* correct this?" And they had the courage to take up the torch, to speak the word, to do the deed. Moses, Isaiah, Jesus, Peter, Paul, Luther, Wesley, Mother Teresa—all these, and many more like them, saw a problem and heard God calling them to do something about it. Each responded creatively and courageously to the question, "Why not you?"

Do you know what it means every time you see a situation that needs correcting, or a job that needs to be done, or a person who needs to be helped? It means that God is calling you to do something. If you see it, then that is God's way of calling you. God is asking, "Why don't you do something about this? Why don't you right this wrong? Why don't you make this world a better place? Why not you?"

Are You Able to Bend Without Breaking?

One of Aesop's fables told of a mighty oak tree and a humble reed, growing side by side on the edge of a river. From time to time they spoke to each other, but they were not close friends because the mighty oak considered itself far superior to the humble reed and looked down upon the reed from a great height.

"You have no pride," the oak told the reed. "You bend and bow to the lightest breeze. You should be more dignified and proud, like me. You should stand erect, as I do. No wind can make me stoop or lower myself."

Just then a fierce storm sprang up. Lightning flashed and strong winds blew so hard they shook the trees. The unbending oak stood firm for a while. But the oak's very stiffness was its undoing. The storm struck hard against the oak, tore its branches, broke its biggest boughs, and toppled it into the river. Meanwhile, the reed swayed and bent, letting the wind blow over it, but the reed did not break. When the storm passed, the reed sprang back and was still growing on the edge of the river!

In this ancient fable, a valuable Christian quality is portrayed in a graphic way. That quality is *resilience*—the strength to bend without breaking. The dictionary defines *resilience* as the ability to spring back, to return to the original form or position after being bent or compressed; buoyancy; the ability to recover readily from illness, depression, or adversity; the strength to withstand shock without permanent damage.

To clarify it further, let me tell you what resilience is *not!:*

- It is not brittleness or self-pity.
- It is not intolerance or closed-mindedness.
- It is not legalism or a holier than thou attitude.
- It is not resentment or bitterness.

Resilience is openness; it is the strength to bend without breaking. Psychologists are writing a great deal today about mental health, and they are emphasizing the need for a resiliency of spirit—a spirit that will bend as a reed bends with the wind but will not break. The manufacturers of automobile tires first tried to make a tire that would resist the shocks of the road, but that tire was soon cut to pieces, torn to shreds. Then they started to make tires that would give a little and absorb the shocks. Those tires are still with us; they have endured because they are resilient; they give, they absorb, and they bounce back.

In like manner, we need to learn how to take the storms of life with resilience, rather than with resentment or self-pity. The storms do come, the winds do blow, the rains do fall, and the quality of resilience can serve us well in the living of these days:

First, we can be resilient in disappointment.

Disappointment is a fact of life. There is no escape. At one time or another, all of us know the pain and heartache of disappointment. Resilient people bounce back and, with the help of God, turn their disappointments into victories.

Second, we can be resilient in our service.

Our calling is to serve God with all we have, wherever we may be. We can't always choose our place of service. We can't all be officers or presidents or bishops or governors or soloists. Besides, there are no perfect situations for serving. So bounce back and love God and serve God wherever you are.

Third, we can be resilient in our thinking.

Most of us need help here. It is so easy to be brittle, hard, closedminded and unbending in our thinking. We need to remember that the mind is like a parachute; it works best when open!

Fourth, we can be resilient in our relations with others.

Resilience is one of the faces of love; it is the ability to give in, not always to demand our own way; it is the strength of

73

understanding and compassion and forgiveness—and we could all use a lot of that!

Can Success Be Dangerous?

Our own successes can ruin us, if we are not careful. They can make us lazy or spoiled or complacent or afraid—afraid to take new steps, to try new things, to risk new challenges, afraid to think new thoughts.

Wasn't that the rich young ruler's problem? His "success" made him unable to respond to Jesus' call. His success made him afraid to try something new. His success caused him to "turn away sorrowfully."

There is an ancient legend about the flute that Moses played as he tended his flocks upon the plains of Midian. Just before his death, Moses gave the flute to the priests, and on high occasions, they would play it in worship services. It was a simple inexpensive shepherd's flute, but it had a beautiful tone.

After some years, it was decided that Moses' flute should be more beautiful and ornate, so it was covered with gold and inlaid jewels. When the decorations were finished, the flute was beautiful, but there was only one thing wrong—it would not play a note! It was externally beautiful, but it would not work anymore! This legend has a powerful message for us—that we can be immobilized by our past successes if we dwell on them too much.

I don't know a lot about the sport of boxing, but I know enough to understand two phrases that TV fight analysts use—phrases that carry over into other dimensions of life. A former boxer, talking about an upcoming fight, used these two phrases. First, he predicted that one fighter, who had been very successful, would lose because he had become a "fat cat." Then he predicted that the other boxer would win because he was a "hungry" fighter!

I knew what he meant. Fat cats in any field are those who, because of their past successes, have become spoiled, lazy, complacent, self-satisfied, pompous, prideful. Those in any field who are "hungry" are those who are striving, struggling, working, dreaming, reaching, sacrificing, and willing to pay the price.

As I thought of this, somehow my mind recalled the words of Jesus: "Blessed are those who hunger and thirst for righteousness"; and the words of Paul: "Forgetting what lies behind . . . I press on" (Matt. 5:6; Phil. 3:13 RSV).

Some years ago, William Fisher wrote these words in his book *Don't Park Here:*

> More lives have been shriveled by success than failure! Out of the humiliation of failure can come powerful incentives to try again, to prove one's worth and to verify one's ability. But out of the satisfactions of success too often come a complacency and contentment that lull the mind, erode the will, and cut the nerve of continued effort to achieve.

So many people make the truth of this thought evident:

- the athlete who "relaxes" on her press clippings and loses the sharpness that originally made her great;
- the writer who could be masterful, but settles for mediocrity;
- the politician who starts out to serve the people, but after his early success, wants the people to serve him;
- the student who could be a pace-setter but becomes satisfied simply to pass;

- the artist who achieves greatness, but is caught up in her self-importance and loses her touch;
- the graduate who finished at the top of his class but never measures up to his potential because he dwells on what he has done, rather than on what remains to be done.

Have you considered how easily this can happen in our spiritual lives? So many of us look back on the place, date, and time when we felt some moving experience with God. And this is fine, but we must not be content to park by that experience. We must *press on!* Somehow, we must move on to greater depths of faith and commitment, and that comes only through struggle, discipline, and perseverance. We are always tempted to stop, to quit, to rest on our laurels, but the person of faith never stops. The person of faith sticks it out!

Do You Feel Crammed in a Cage?

The great British preacher W. E. Sangster tells of going to a zoo one day. As he was walking about seeing the sights, he came upon an eagle in a cage. He looked at the eagle; he saw the powerful wings, beautifully feathered wings meant for the skies, meant for flying. As he stood there, someone in the crowd expressed aloud what he was feeling. "Made for the skies and crammed in a cage."

Think about that phrase for a moment: "Made for the skies and crammed in a cage." There is a powerful message here. That phrase brings many different images to my mind.

I think of the apostle Paul, writing to the Christians in Rome: "Don't let the world around you squeeze you into its mold" (Rom. 12:2 Phillips). Isn't that just another way of saying, "You are made for the skies, so don't let the world cram you into a cage"?

I think of Soren Kierkegaard, the respected Danish theologian, and his story about the wild duck flying south for the winter. The duck saw an abundant supply of corn in a barnyard, so it swooped down, took a closer look, and decided to spend the winter eating corn in that barnyard. Then in the spring, when the other wild ducks flew over, heading north, the wild duck tried to fly up and join its friends, but, it couldn't get off the ground. It had become too fat, too tame, too domesticated. So it remained trapped in the boredom of the barnyard, imprisoned by its own greed and laziness. The wild duck was made for the skies, but it was crammed into a cage of its own making.

I think of Harry Emerson Fosdick, the famous pastor of Riverside Church in New York City, and his fascinating story about a vulture. It was a wintry day on the Niagara River below Buffalo, New York. The bird of prey lighted on a carcass floating down the river and began to feed. It intended to feed as long as it could and then to fly to safety just above the falls. But when the vulture tried to fly away, its claws had become frozen to the carcass it was feeding on. And the vulture plunged over the falls to its death. The vulture was made for the skies, but it was crammed into a cage of its own making, imprisoned by the clutch of its claws.

Like the vulture, our hands freeze to that which we feed upon, and though we are meant for the skies, we are crammed into a cage.

- If we are self-centered, we are crammed into the cage of selfishness!

- If we feed on defeat, we are crammed into the cage of negativism.
- If we are hooked on alcohol or drugs or tranquilizers, we are crammed into the cage of escapism.
- If we always maintain the status quo, we are crammed into the cage of a closed mind.
- If we are jealous or resentful, we are crammed into the cage of hate.
- If we constantly talk about other people, we are crammed into the cage of gossip.
- If we are anxiety-ridden, we are crammed into the cage of fear.

If we are frozen in one of those attitude,s we are headed for a fall! We have lost our freedom! We are made for the skies, but we have been crammed into a cage. Many people do let one little thing eclipse their lives and enslave them—things like prejudice or envy or a bad temper or a worried spirit or nervous tension or hostility.

What about you? Is there anything in your life that's making a slave of you? You were made for the skies, you were meant for greatness, but are you letting something imprison you? Are you letting stubborn pride, or selfishness, or prejudice, or hate, or jealousy, or apathy cram you into a cage? It's something to think about, isn't it?

What Is Consecrated Stubbornness?

The Academy Award winning film *Chariots of Fire* is the story of Eric Liddell's "consecrated stubbornness," his unbending commitment, his firm refusal to compromise his principles.

Eric Liddell was born in the Orient, the son of Christian missionaries from Scotland. After returning to Scotland for his education, Liddell became one of Scotland's most distinguished and respected athletes, first as a rugby player and later as a sprinter. The missionary society sensed his unique abilities as a runner, and encouraged him to train for the Olympics.

"We need some muscular Christians!" they said. "Your athletic achievements will enhance your witness and open doors for you to proclaim your message. You must run—not for personal glory, but to honor God!"

So Eric Liddell ran. My, how he ran! With reckless abandon, he ran! Every day, he ran—every day, that is, except Sunday. He never ran on Sunday. He never trained on Sunday. He never exercised on Sunday, because that is God's day. He had been taught that from childhood, and it had become a significant principle in his faith pilgrimage, an important part of his faith experience.

Eric Liddell was selected to run in the 100-meter dash for the United Kingdom in the Olympic Games, to be held in Paris that year. When the time came, Liddell was primed and ready. Hopes were high that he could bring a gold medal back to his native land.

However, en route to Paris, Eric Liddell heard something that just couldn't be true. It couldn't be—but it was. The qualifying heat for the 100-meter dash was to be held on a Sunday. Now, Liddell wanted, more than we can imagine, to run in the Olympic Games. It was the moment he had dreamed of and worked for and anticipated.

But he refused to run on Sunday. For him, that would be a betrayal of his commitment to God. He refused to compromise his principles. He refused to water down his commitment. He refused to rationalize his conscience. To run on Sunday would be a contradiction of what he was there for, because he was there to honor God.

The qualifying heat was indeed held on a Sunday, and Eric Liddell stubbornly refused to run. But if you will look at the Olympic records, you will find the name of Eric Liddell. He ran later in the week, on Friday, in the 400-meter dash—a race he had not trained for, a race in which he had not competed before in international competition. And he not only won, but set a new Olympic record.

But Eric Liddell is not remembered because he won an Olympic race. Many have done that. Rather, he is remembered because he, like many great people before him, stubbornly refused to compromise his commitment to God.

After the Olympics, Eric Liddell became a missionary to China. He joins a marvelous line of committed people who became a great inspiration to the world because they refused to sell out or compromise their principles.

- There is Peter, saying, "We must obey God rather than men!"

- There is Luther, saying, "I will not recant. Here I stand, I can do no other!"

- There is Jesus, saying, "Not my will, Father, but thine be done!"

These great personalities offer dramatic proof that sometimes we must take a stand for what we believe—even when it is hard to do—and trust God to make it come out right. Every now and then, all of us need a little "consecrated stubbornness."

Are Some Things Worth Saying Again and Again?

Some things are worth repeating. Some things are worth saying again and again—and worth hearing again and again.

Benjamin Franklin believed this when he published the first edition of *Poor Richard's Almanac* in 1733 and continued to publish it for twenty-six years. Poor Richard had all the usual features of almanacs, including astrological predictions, jokes, verses, and fiction. But Franklin's almanac was most famous for its wise sayings. Franklin himself said that he "assembled the wisdom of many ages and nations" into these proverbs, which he obviously felt were worth saying again and again. Some were wise, some were witty—and some were both:

- God helps them that help themselves.
- A penny saved is a penny earned.
- Little strokes fell great oaks.
- He's a fool that makes his doctor his heir.
- He that falls in love with himself will have no rivals.

Wise sayings like these have been with us since the beginning of time. Old proverbs, short picturesque sentences which tell a helpful truth or some bit of useful wisdom, seem to be a part of every language and every people's heritage. Thousands of years ago, Cicero gave us some words that have been repeated millions of times since he first spoke them: One does not need to believe everything one hears; virtue is its own reward.

The Old Testament contains an entire book of proverbs and additional wisdom literature—fascinating sayings that have been handed down from generation to generation: A soft answer turns away wrath; The fear of the Lord is the beginning of wisdom; A good name is to be chosen rather than great riches. The Ten Commandments are, in a sense, wise sayings which Moses and the early Israelites felt were worth repeating, worth saying again and again, and worth hearing again and again.

Nowadays, in contemporary ways, we still pass on ideas we want repeated—in graffiti, on billboards, commercials, banners, and bumper stickers:

- Today is the first day of the rest of your life.
- Make my words sweet and tender today, for I may have to eat them tomorrow.
- Lord, teach me to be patient right now!
- Love makes the world go 'round.

As we recognize the importance of proverbs and wise sayings, and the significance they have played in the history of humankind, it's interesting to look back at the teachings of Jesus, to discover what key ideas he felt were worth repeating. I did this recently and noticed that three major thoughts emerged again and again.

First, people are more important than things.

Jesus underscored that point repeatedly. People matter! he said to us. People are more important than ritual, more important than sacrifice, more important than laws or systems, more important than things. According to Jesus, things are to be used and people are to be loved. That phrase must be repeated, because we are prone not only to forget it, but to reverse it, tending to use people and love things. But Jesus brings us up short by saying it again and again: People are more important than things. The best way to show our love for God is to love one another.

Second, discipleship is costly.

Again and again Jesus told us that discipleship is costly. You can't be a person of faith and live by the law of selfishness. That's a contradiction. Discipleship means dying to selfishness and coming alive to self-givingness. "Deny yourself . . . take up your cross . . . count the cost . . . follow me." The price is high, but it's worth it. As someone put it, "The only thing more costly than caring is not caring!"

Third, God loves us.

God is not an angry, hostile, vindictive deity who must be appeased. More than anything else, this is what Jesus came to teach us. He did not come to change God's mind, but to reveal it. Again and again he painted God's portrait with strokes of love as gracious, merciful, forgiving, compassionate. That is good news, and it's worth saying and hearing again and again.

Is It Sinful to Be Angry?

It was late on a Monday afternoon. I was going through some things on my desk when I sensed someone's presence. Have you ever had that experience? My back was to the door and I was absorbed in what I was doing, when suddenly I felt the presence of another person. I turned around, and there at the door to my office stood a young woman. She was crying quietly.

She said, "Jim, I'm sorry about walking in like this, but I just had to talk to somebody." She went on to describe a family squabble that had erupted over nothing really important. It could have been avoided or handled differently, she admitted, but it hadn't been. And angry, hostile words and actions had exploded.

"I got so mad," she said. "I was so angry that I lost control. I couldn't see straight. I lost my head, and now I'm so ashamed. I feel devastated."

She paused for a moment and then went on, "Is it sinful to get angry? It must be, because my soul feels so deflated and empty after my angry outburst."

Then she added, "Sometimes I feel as if God had converted every part of me except my temper. I'm a Christian, and I try to do what is right, but I must confess that I have a terrible temper. I can get *so* angry!"

Well, what do you think? What would you have told that young woman? Is it sinful to be angry? One thing is certain: Anger *can* be sinful. It can become a spiritual cancer. It can destroy us and devastate other people. It can disrupt families, ruin friendships, split churches, and start wars. In human nature, anger is a powerful force which, too often, we release toward negative, destructive ends.

In the Sermon on the Mount, Jesus spoke of a forbidden anger. There he condemned anger, but we know that later he himself became angry—angry enough to run the money changers out of the Temple. What are we to make of this? How do we reconcile the two? Was Jesus being inconsistent?

In order to find an answer to these hard questions, we need to recognize the fact that there are several different kinds of anger. Let's take a look at three common varieties and see if we can find ourselves somewhere here.

First, there is "adolescent" anger.

This, unfortunately, is not confined to adolescents. Sadly, grown-ups can have childish temperaments. Psychiatrists tell us that people who are short-tempered, hostile, and irritable are basically immature. They may be adults physically, but emotionally, they may still be little children who want to scream and kick because they can't have their own way:

- There is the man who flies into a rage because his toast is burnt.
- There is the woman who quits the club because her name was accidentally omitted from a list of committee members.
- There is the teenager who runs to her room and slams the door and pouts because she isn't permitted to go to the slumber party.
- There is the church member who quits the church because his announcement was left out of the bulletin.

Does any of this sound familiar? Be honest now. Have you grown up? Or are you still the victim of adolescent anger? What makes you angry—cold coffee? the ring in the bathtub? an improperly squeezed toothpaste tube? a traffic jam? homework? a missed parking place?

Some people show by their tantrums that, quite simply, they have never grown up. Like little children, they have made themselves the center of the universe and when their world is crossed, they get cross! All through the Scriptures, we are warned about the sinful misuse of anger, and we are urged to mature spiritually—to grow up!

Second, there is brooding, seething anger.

We can say, without a doubt, that this kind of anger is sinful because it is anger that seeks vengeance, anger that will not forgive; it is murderous anger. In the Greek language, there are two words for anger: *thumos,* "anger which quickly blazes up and quickly dies down"; and *orgé,* "anger which broods and seethes and looks for the chance to pay somebody back."

Nothing will separate us from God and devastate our souls and bring hell into our lives more quickly than *orgé*. There's no question about it. It is as sinful as sin can be.

Third, there is constructive anger— righteous indignation.

As always, Jesus is our best example of righteous indignation. Two dramatic things can be said about his use of this emotion.

On the one hand, Jesus was never upset by unkindness directed toward himself! He was never personally offended! He was criticized, questioned, rejected, accused falsely, lied about, pushed and shoved, taunted, beaten, spat upon, cursed at, and nailed to a cross. But "when he was reviled, he reviled not again" (I Peter 2:23 KJV). They did all that, and when they finished, he said, "Father, forgive them!"

Let me add a quick note here. This does not mean that we should permit anyone to abuse us. If we are in an abusive situation, we should report that and get out of it as soon as possible. I am simply saying that Jesus' anger was never selfish and neither should ours be.

On the other hand, Jesus did become upset by injustices done to others! He was upset when he saw other people being exploited or mistreated or cheated or hurt. When he saw a woman judged without mercy, he was upset. When he saw religious leaders place custom and tradition before human need, he was upset. When he saw people cheated in the Temple, he was so upset that he overturned the money changers' tables and drove them out.

Jesus was never upset by unkindness directed toward himself, but he was upset by injustices directed toward others. Our problem is that, more often than not, we can be personally offended, but fail to see others being exploited or mistreated.

Be honest now. What makes you angry? Someone once said, "You can tell the size of a person by the size of the thing that makes that person mad."

How Does Truth Set You Free?

It was the summer of 1975. Jane was twenty-four years old and she had recently graduated from the University of Texas. Looking through the classified section, she saw a blind advertisement: "Sincere, conscientious person interested in the betterment of mankind, call this number."

Out of curiosity, she picked up the phone and dialed the number. Little did she know that with that phone call, her mind had begun a journey from which it might never return.

Before she realized what was happening, Jane was caught up in a radical youth movement. Through the use of various subtle mind-manipulating techniques—some would call it brainwashing—she was transformed into a kind of obedient, subservient zombie, doing whatever the group commanded.

She was taught that God was replacing Christianity with this radical new youth movement. She was told to forget her family, her friends, her past. At one point, "I felt that someone had placed a psychological bomb on my head, and if I left the group it would explode," she said.

Jane stayed with the group for a couple of months, but toward the end of the summer, she had to return home to handle some unfinished personal business. The day after she arrived, she was eating breakfast when the doorbell rang. Suddenly, a man entered the room and introduced himself as a minister. Jane's parents had asked the minister in to deprogram her.

Jane and the minister argued and debated and yelled at each other for eight hours. He showed her documents which exposed the youth movement and its dangers. He played tapes of other young people who had been deprogrammed, but nothing penetrated her confused mind.

Then the minister did something that broke through. He reached over, picked up a Bible and turned to the eighth chapter of John's Gospel. Then he quietly read these words of Jesus: "You will know the truth and the truth will set you free!"

"The truth will set you free"—those words exploded into Jane's mind. She said it was as though suddenly a light had been turned on in the room, and a tremendous burden was lifted from her shoulders. For the first time since joining the cult, she felt free, really free!

The months that followed were hard for Jane. She said it was like adjusting to another planet or withdrawing from a drug. She had to learn to think all over again. During those difficult days, the one thing that kept her going was that verse of Scripture: "You will know the truth and the truth will set you free" (*Time* Magazine, June 14, 1976; I have not used Jane's real name here).

I hope that none of us will ever experience what Jane went through, but the point is that the truth of Christ can indeed set us free from those things that ensnare us, encumber us, or imprison us. This is a dominant theme in the Scriptures. Zacchaeus was set free from his greed and loneliness. The woman at the well was set free from her sordid past. The woman accused of adultery was set free from her moral dilemma.

I don't know if there is something that is locking you up. Maybe it's greed or selfishness; maybe it's pride or vanity; maybe it's resentment or jealousy; maybe it's fear or prejudice. But I do know that Christ has the key, and he can set you free! No matter what it is, the truth of Christ can set you free!

In one of his imaginative tales, Lewis Carroll writes about a lock that runs around frantically, rushes to and fro in a panic.

"What's the matter?" someone asks.

The lock answers, "I am seeking someone to unlock me!"

Isn't that true of all of us? We are seeking someone to unlock us. We want to be free to live zestfully and celebrate life, but somehow we feel like zombies, programmed to go through the motions—locked up and sealed off from real, vibrant living.

The good news of our faith is that the truth of Christ can set us free from anything that's imprisoning us, because Christ shows us two tremendously important things. He shows us what God is like, and he shows us what God wants us to be like—love. Nothing is more freeing than that—to realize that God is loving and that God wants us to be loving! That truth sets us free!

Can You Remember to Forget?

A good memory is a wonderful gift! Most of us wish we could improve our memories. How terrific it would be, we think, to have an infallible memory, an instant recall of all former impressions.

The truth is that there aren't many people with photographic memories. In fact, most of us suffer from memories that fail us at the most inopportune times. Some poet once said this about the mind:

The only time it ever sits down
Is when I stand up to speak!

As important as a good memory may be, however, the power to forget may be equally valuable. On first thought, most of us may believe that we need no help in the forgetting department. We forget names, appointments, addresses, dates, even words; and the result is often embarrassing and frustrating. As troublesome as this is, though, it is still a good thing to forget some things. With that in mind, consider these vignettes:

- Two people are talking—
    First Person: "My friend has a terrible memory, the worst memory I ever heard of."
    Second Person: "Forgets everything, huh?"
    First Person: "No! *Remembers* everything!"
- Clara Barton, founder of the American Red Cross, was once reminded of a cruelty done to her. Serenely, she replied, "I distinctly remember forgetting that!"
- Dr. John Scales once said to me, "My father taught me that one of God's greatest blessings is the ability to forget some things and go on with life."
- The apostle Paul knew that there are some things you should forget, and he made it clear in his letter to the Philippians: "Forgetting those things that are past. Forgetting what lies behind . . . I press on!" Paul had learned that as wonderful as it is to remember, it is also sometimes good to intentionally forget.

Let me illustrate this by underscoring some specific things that we may want to remember to forget.

First, we may need to forget our past accomplishments.

Past victories, if we dwell on them, can make us lazy, spoiled, or complacent. It's not healthy to live in the glow of past successes for too long. We must constantly press ahead, looking for new thresholds and new challenges.

Second, we may need to forget our past hurts.

Past hurts can dampen our spirits, drain away our energies, and poison our souls. In other words, Don't nurse grievances! Don't give in to self-pity! Don't wallow in your heartaches! Put them behind you—and go on with life.

Third, we may need to forget our failures.

One song put it this way: "You can pick yourself up, dust yourself off, and start all over again." No failure need be final. We can start over, make a new beginning, try again.

Several years ago, a newspaper reporter asked an eminent psychologist, "What do you try to do for those who come to you for treatment?"

The psychologist answered, "Our objective is to free the patient from the tyranny of the past."

How important that is! All of us have past failures that haunt us, but we don't need to be defeated by them. No one who can say, "I'd like to try again" is ever a failure! The point to remember is that poor memory is not always bad. There are some things we need to purposefully forget.

Is Your Faith Too Small?

In 1650, Oliver Cromwell sent his famous message to the General Assembly of the Church of Scotland. It contained these words: "I beseech you . . . to think it possible that you may be mistaken"! Then he urged them to read chapter 28 of Isaiah. He wanted them to learn there the futility of "little religion" or "small faith." In that chapter, the prophet Isaiah uses a colorful illustration to drive home his point: "The bed you have made is far too short to lie on; and the blankets are too narrow to cover you."

With this humorous figure of the too-short bed and the too-narrow covers, Isaiah is raising some haunting questions for all of us: Is our religion too little? Is our thinking too narrow? Is our faith big enough? Or is it too small?

Anyone who has ever spent a restless night on a short, uncomfortable bed or tried to make it through a freezing night with inadequate covers knows what Isaiah is pointing out here. We know that such conditions make us miserable. Isaiah said that this is the way of people whose faith is too small—they are cold, restless, dissatisfied. And that is what Isaiah saw in his people. Their faith was too small, elaborate ceremony without moral content, an empty religion with shallow faith.

Isaiah knew that this kind of empty religion might serve those who "sunned themselves" in the warmth of momentary prosperity. But when night fell, and the cold, frigid, blustering, howling winds of trouble struck, it would be inadequate. Isaiah is suggesting that each of us needs to examine our faith to see whether it is equal to the demands of life.

Well, how is it with you? Is your faith big enough? Or is it too small? Let's check ourselves by looking at some specific measuring sticks.

First, your faith is too small if it
makes you satisfied with your spiritual attainment.

Good religion keeps on growing; it is always open to new truths from God. When we become self-satisfied or lazy or complacent, then our faith is too small.

Second, your faith is too small
if it makes you critical of others.

Something is wrong with your religion if it makes you holier than thou, if it causes you to pass judgment on others, or if it causes you to feel that every person who does not agree with your theology is wrong or lost. Actually, genuine faith works in just the opposite way. It makes you more loving, rather than more critical.

Third, your faith is too small
if it changes you outwardly, but not inwardly.

We can do the right things for the wrong reasons. We can do something that looks good and, at the same time, be seething inside. If our motivations and inner attitudes are not right, then our faith is too small.

Fourth, your faith is too small
if it doesn't work in practical, day-to-day living.

Genuine faith works *now*. Genuine religion touches our lives, our attitudes, our values, our morality, our relationships, *now*. It makes us better people *now*. It is not an insurance policy for another day, but a life-style that enables us to celebrate the present.

Some years ago, Dr. Harry Emerson Fosdick received a letter from a young mother in which she told of moving into a new subdivision just outside New York City:

Dr. Fosdick, we tried everything we could think of to make this place something other than a real-estate development. We tried organized recreation, community picnics, and square dancing. We formed a woman's club and held bridge parties and started a garden club. We had a parents' organization and evening discussion groups. We tried everything. But it was not until the church came that we changed from a subdivision into a community and became real neighbors.

The point is that faith (the church) does work in practical day-to-day living. Though the other activities did not create a real community, the church did.

Genuine faith works *now*. It gives you a sense of partnership with God and people, and there is nothing small about that.

Why Am I Important?

This letter was written by Dr. Moore to his daughter upon her graduation from high school.

Dear Jodi,

Let me take this occasion to express what your mother and I have felt since the day you were born—namely, that we love you more than words could ever express!

We are so proud of you! We are proud of your accomplishments, but most of all, we are proud of who you are! You are beautiful—inside and out!

You are so special, and sometimes you amaze us with your emotional and spiritual maturity. You are wise and understanding and compassionate beyond your years.

We are so grateful to God for you. We always have been and always will be thankful for the love and joy and excitement that you have brought into our lives.

You have so many rare and wonderful gifts and talents. You can do and be anything you want to be, and as we have discussed before, the key is to aim high and to always be the best person you can be.

You are bright, beautiful, capable, conscientious, personable, friendly, sensitive, and thoughtful, but most of all, you are kind! And that makes us so proud of you. As a matter of fact, you are one of the most tender, caring persons we have ever met, and nothing could please us more.

Over the years, we have known and seen many young people who were outstanding. I used to think, "Wouldn't it be great if we could have a daughter like that!" And now we do—and then some! The frosting on the cake for us is that, out of all those great young people we have known and respected and appreciated, you, in our eyes, outshine them all—and you are ours! I wanted to write this letter to say that to you. I've been telling everybody that "I know you!" and that we are rich in the things that count most!

My prayer for you and your future is that God will continue to use you as a peacemaker, as the instrument of his love, as the vessel of his kindness—and that he will bless you with the best things of life, which I feel you so richly deserve.

Love,
Dad

P.S. If you ever need an understanding friend or a sympathetic ear, your folks are available . . . and so is your little brother.